The BENGHAZI
HOAX

David Brock, Ari Rabin-Havt & Media Matters for America

The Hoaxsters

Senator Kelly Ayotte, *R-NH*

Eric Bolling, Host, *Fox News Channel*

Ambassador John Bolton, *Fox News Contributor,*
Foreign Policy Advisor Romney/Ryan 2012

Gretchen Carlson, Host, *Fox News Channel*

Representative Jason Chaffetz, *R-UT*

Lanhee Chen, Foreign Policy Advisor, *Romney/Ryan 2012*

Joseph diGenova, Attorney

Steve Doocy, Host, *Fox News Channel*

Senator Lindsay Graham, *R-SC*

Sean Hannity, Host, *Fox News Channel*

Representative Darrell Issa, *R-CA,*
Chairman, *House Committee on Oversight & Government Reform*

Brian Kilmeade, Host, *Fox News Channel*

Senator John McCain, *R-AZ*

Mitt Romney, Former Governor of Massachusetts,
2012 Republican Presidential Nominee

Stuart Stevens, Senior Advisor, *Romney/Ryan 2012*

Contents

Introduction: Romney's Dilemma

Mitt Romney woke up on the morning of September 11, 2012, with big hopes for this day — that he'd stop the slow slide of his campaign for the presidency. The political conventions were in his rear-view mirror, and the Republican nominee for the White House was trailing President Obama in most major polls. In an ABC News/*Washington Post* poll released at the start of the week, the former Massachusetts governor's previous 1-point lead had flipped to a 6-point deficit.[1]

"Mr. Obama almost certainly had the more successful convention than Mr. Romney," wrote Nate Silver, the polling guru and then-*New York Times* blogger.[2] While the incumbent's gathering in Charlotte was marked by party unity and rousing testimonials from Obama's wife, Michelle, and former President Bill Clinton, Romney's confab in Tampa had fallen flat. One of the biggest problems, according to critics in the media, was a glaring omission in Romney's acceptance speech: The candidate's failure to make even a passing mention of the U.S. troops still fighting and dying overseas in Afghanistan. Even some of Romney's conservative supporters were flabbergasted. *Weekly Standard* editor William Kristol wrote Romney's failure to praise and acknowledge the troops was not just "an error" but "a failure of civic responsibility."[3]

Now, on September 11, the 11th anniversary of the Al Qaeda terrorist attacks on United States soil, the Romney camp had a unique — but complicated — opportunity for a do-over. The candidate was slated to speak before the National Guard Association convention in Reno, Nevada — an ideal gathering for discussing respect for military service while touching on his ideas for veterans' affairs and the use of American forces overseas. At the same time, there was a limit on what he could say: the candidates had agreed to halt all negative campaigning for the 24 hours of the 9/11 anniversary.[4]

The New York Times later reported that Romney "said that while he would normally offer a contrasting vision with President Obama's on national security and the military, 'There is a time and a place for that, but this day is not that. It is instead a day to express gratitude to the men and women who have fought — and who are still fighting — to protect us and our country, including those who traced the trail of terror to that walled compound in Abbottabad and the SEALs who delivered justice to Osama bin Laden.'"[5]

Roughly 7,000 miles away, a U.S. compound was coming under siege. The city of Benghazi in eastern Libya had been at the vanguard of the uprising against longtime Libyan dictator Moammar Gadhafi, and now it was home to an American diplomatic facility that had been targeted for attack. Shortly after 9 p.m. local time – or 3 p.m. in the eastern United States – a Toyota pickup truck belonging to militia members thought to be friendly to American interests pulled up to the front entrance of the compound. The pickup, with anti-aircraft guns mounted in the back, startled the guard on duty by peeling out, throwing up gravel as it vanished into the desert night. It was the last and most dramatic sign that something was amiss that day.

Sean Smith, the 34-year-old chief information officer for the consulate posting – a computer whiz and a tireless gamer – had been online with a gaming friend when he signed off, "Assuming we don't die tonight. We saw one of the 'police' that guard our compound taking pictures." Now, hours later, Smith was back online when he heard a disturbance near the front gate. "Fuck," he wrote. "Gunfire."[6] What would transpire in the eastern Libyan city during a long and hellish night was an American tragedy that ended in the deaths of Smith, two other U.S. security personnel, and this country's ambassador to Libya, J. Christopher Stevens. Stevens was a remarkable 52-year-old American – a former Peace Corps member who'd abandoned a likely lucrative law career to represent the United States and promote its ideals in dangerous postings abroad.

No one could have imagined how quickly the murder of Stevens and three other Americans would become politicized by a hungry right-wing leviathan of savage punditry and pseudo-journalism. Nor could anyone fathom how the most basic facts would get twisted, contorted, and even invented out of thin air to create bogus narratives – first to suggest that a U.S. president seeking re-election was incompetent, feckless, or sympathetic to terror, and then, when that faltered, to tarnish the reputation of his secretary of state as the public speculated she might run for president in 2016.

Had the Benghazi attack not occurred at this unique moment – on a day when the Republican candidate for the presidency and his promoters in the conservative media were desperate for a new storyline, especially one that would undercut the popular effect of the raid that killed Osama bin Laden the year before – this tragedy might not have been converted into a political scandal. After all, Benghazi was just one of at least 157 attacks on our diplomatic facilities over a 15-year period, 9 of which resulted in U.S. fatalities.[7] That Benghazi would remain at the forefront of the contentious American political conversation for the next year, and likely beyond, speaks less to any special circumstances of the September 11, 2012, attack, and more to the insidious nature of a Republican noise machine that has grown in size – as well as decibels – over the last four decades.

In fact, what has been called "the Benghazi scandal" by a chorus of voices including Fox News, right-wing radio talkers like Rush Limbaugh and Sean Hannity, and sympathetic websites like the Drudge Report, is better described as the Benghazi hoax. The act of terror that killed four Americans has become what the late film director Alfred Hitchcock would have called a "MacGuffin" – an obscure plot driver whose real significance derives from the way that it motivates the characters. In this case, those characters are the ones who must fill an hour or an afternoon of airtime with partisan vitriol and hyperbole, and the Republicans in charge of investigative committees empowered to find a scandal – any kind of scandal – inside a Democratic White House.

To create a political hoax using a terrorist assault that killed Americans is, of course, unconscionable, but it has also served as a harmful national distraction. What should have been a tightly focused investigation into the protection of U.S. diplomatic posts and our policy in Libya has been hijacked by unfounded and sometimes wild conspiracy theories that have diverted attention from real issues that affect American voters. Over months, manufactured right-wing narratives bled slowly into news coverage from mainstream journalists eager to show their "balanced" approach – thus misleading citizens who pay only casual attention to political developments.

The endurance of the Benghazi storyline – even as myth after myth has been debunked – helps explain why the GOP spin factory seems determined to keep Benghazi alive as a political attack until the 2016 presidential election, if possible. The hidden saga of how this hoax perpetuates itself is revealing in its outbreaks of sheer buffoonery. But it should be mostly infuriating for anyone who cares about the state of political discourse in America.

The decisions that launched the Benghazi hoax and caused it to eventually metastasize took place before the night of September 11 was even over.

The GOP nominee was flying back across the country on the campaign's McDonnell Douglas MD-83, en route from Nevada to the key battle-ground state of Florida, when news reached Romney's advisers that at least one American had died in Libya. A group of Romney's aides, including policy director Lanhee Chen, media strategist Stuart Stevens, and foreign policy adviser and former Ambassador Richard Williamson, convened on a conference call to draft a statement. Without even knowing the details of a tragedy, Romney's team saw opportunity.[8]

It had only been a couple of hours since the candidate had declared that the September 11 anniversary was not "a time and a place" for a contrasting vision on foreign affairs – but suddenly the chance to dent Obama's terrorism *bona fides* established in the 2011 bin Laden raid was too tempting.

But the initial information coming out of the Middle East was also very confusing – and not just because of the late hour and the still-unfolding situation at the Benghazi compound. September 11, 2012, had been a day of chaos across the Islamic world. Outside the U.S. Embassy in Cairo, the largest city in the Arab world, about 3,000 protestors condemned *Innocence of Muslims*, a poorly produced American-made video posted to YouTube that mocked the Prophet Muhammad. By day's end in the Egyptian capital, Islamist militants breached the walls of the diplomatic complex; the U.S. flag was torn down and an Islamist black flag was raised in its place.

Over the next several weeks, heated anti-American demonstrations were staged in response to the video in more than 20 countries, including outside U.S. embassies and consulates in Tunisia, Yemen, Pakistan, and Afghanistan. Across the Middle East, Africa, and South Asia, there were numerous reports of fatalities (although none involving Americans).[9]

The video at the center of the protests had been produced by Nakoula Basseley Nakoula, an Egyptian Coptic Christian, and by a right-wing American evangelical Christian named Steve Klein who has been linked to Islamophobic groups. Nakoula was a murky character; in 2010, he had pleaded no contest to bank fraud charges after opening fraudulent accounts using stolen Social Security numbers. He would be arrested again soon after the protests for probation violations. In November 2012, he pled guilty and was sentenced to one year in prison.[10]

His video – really just a short trailer for a supposed longer film that was never released – seemed designed to aim at little besides agitating Muslims. Here's how *Vanity Fair* reviewed it: "Exceptionally amateurish, with disjointed dialogue, jumpy editing, and performances that would have looked melodramatic even in a silent movie, the clip is clearly designed to offend Muslims, portraying Mohammed as a bloodthirsty murderer and Lothario and pedophile with omnidirectional sexual appetites."[11] Yet the reaction to the movie trailer spread around the globe.

The embassy in Cairo, led by Ambassador Anne Patterson, a career diplomat who had previously been appointed ambassador to Pakistan by George W. Bush, made a decision to take action on its own. It released a statement "condemn[ing] the continuing efforts by misguided individuals to hurt the religious feelings of Muslims – as we condemn efforts to offend believers of all religions." The statement continued, "Respect for religious beliefs is a cornerstone of American democracy. We firmly reject the actions by those who abuse the universal right of free speech to hurt the religious beliefs of others."[12]

News of the Cairo statement began to circulate through the media not long before the first news flashes out of Benghazi, where the shots that information officer Smith had first reported were devolving into a noisy attack as a large, growing fire illuminated the night sky. The implication seemed clear at the time: The protests over the YouTube video had deteriorated and spread, from the embassy wall that had been breached in Egypt to an all-out attack in neighboring Libya.

As the Romney plane neared Jacksonville, the magnitude of the news overseas met a desire for a rapid response. The campaign's senior team closely vetted a statement, settling on final language; landing in Florida, the candidate was briefed on developments in Libya and personally approved the release.

Moments later, it was emailed to the media. It was originally embargoed for roughly 90 minutes, until after midnight on the East Coast, to allow his team to claim that they had technically avoided violating the unspoken agreement barring attacks on September 11. But that would be too late for local newscasts or deadline at many newspapers. The anxious Romney campaign lifted that embargo at 10:24 p.m. Eastern time.

"I'm outraged by the attacks on American diplomatic missions in Libya and Egypt and by the death of an American consulate worker in Benghazi," the statement read. "It's disgraceful that the Obama administration's first response was not to condemn attacks on our diplomatic missions, but to sympathize with those who waged the attacks."[13]

The crucial word was "sympathize." Obama had sought the White House in 2008 by offering himself and his policies as the antidote to the harm to America's global reputation caused by the controversial anti-terrorism tactics of George W. Bush and Dick Cheney. Obama's predecessors had invaded Iraq on flimsy pretenses, ordered interrogations of terrorism suspects using techniques the United States has long considered torture, and established indefinite detention without trial for inmates at a prison camp in Guantanamo Bay.

In 2008, then-candidate Obama stood before the Democratic National Convention in Denver and accused the GOP of squandering the nation's diplomatic legacy, promising to "restore our moral standing so that America is once again that last, best hope for all who are called to the cause of freedom, who long for lives of peace, and who yearn for a better future." Just months after taking office, Obama traveled to Cairo to amplify this message before a predominantly Muslim audience. "America is not — and never will be — at war with Islam," he said that day, but he added this caveat: "We will, however, relentlessly confront violent extremists who pose a grave threat to our security — because we reject the same thing that people of all faiths reject: the killing of innocent men, women and children. And it is my first duty as president to protect the American people."[14]

In seeking to create a new tone in U.S. relations with the Arab world, Obama never uttered specific words of apology for what had transpired during the Bush-Cheney years. Yet as soon as these words left the president's mouth, they were enshrined in the right-wing media as an "apology tour" by the likes of former Bush strategist Karl Rove and Rush Limbaugh, who called the Cairo speech "outrageous" and "absurd."[15] As Romney – looking to gain support with ultra-conservative GOP primary voters despite his centrist record as governor of Massachusetts – tightened his hold on the party's nomination, he did not repudiate this extreme, factually challenged rhetoric; instead, Romney made this false premise a centerpiece of his campaign. "I will not and I will never apologize for America," the former Massachusetts governor said in February 2011. "I don't apologize for America, because I believe in America."

The Washington Post's fact-checker had responded to this statement by Romney, and similar ones by his Republican primary rivals, by awarding it Four Pinocchios – the highest rating for dishonesty. "The apology tour never happened," wrote the Post's Glenn Kessler.[16] This admonition clearly had little impact on Romney, who doubled down by titling his obligatory campaign biography *No Apology: The Case for American Greatness* – a rebuttal to a statement that had never been uttered in the first place.

This helps explain why Team Romney was chomping at the bit to release a statement critical of Obama – even if that meant violating the widely lauded one-day truce in negative campaigning. The Romney brain trust had convinced themselves that in this new Cairo statement they had uncovered – retroactively – the proof of the Obama "apology tour." And as a result of what they believed was the Obama administration's fecklessness, an American in the neighboring nation of Libya was now dead.

But there is an even deeper psychological level for understanding the urgency of this critical initial attack by Romney. Since Obama first emerged in 2008 as a favorite for the White House, conservatives would not, and realistically could not, overtly go after a groundbreaking African-American politician over his race. Instead, they hinted that Barack Hussein Obama – the son of a black Muslim from Kenya (and a white anthropologist with deep family roots in Kansas) – couldn't defend America because on some fundamental level he didn't understand the nation that he now commanded. In July 2012, a top surrogate for the Romney campaign, the former George H.W. Bush aide John Sununu, famously told a conference call that the 44th president of the United States needed "to learn how to be an American."[17]

The only thing unusual about the Sununu remark was that it came from such a high-level figure. The notion that Obama was in some way fundamentally un-American festered in the lower rungs of the conservative movement — most famously in the birther movement that scoured the globe for non-existent evidence that the Hawaii native was actually born outside of the United States, rendering him ineligible to serve. Throughout Obama's first term, leading conservatives seized on any statement from Obama or White House aides that didn't describe terrorists or possible terrorist incidents in the starkest, most apocalyptic terms as a sign of his weakness. Their goal: tapping into the absurd subconscious notion that America's commander-in-chief sympathized with America's enemies.

By the late summer of 2012, the Obama-ordered killing of bin Laden and successful strikes against other Al Qaeda leaders had already made a mockery of such attacks. But now, in these first few confused hours, the muddled information coming out of Egypt and Libya certainly looked to Republicans like an opportunity to renew the warped old line of thinking.

Meanwhile, Obama's Pentagon, State Department, and CIA were still in the middle of a long night trying to figure out how to save Americans under fire halfway around the world. The gunfire that Smith reported to his friend was just the opening salvo in an all-out assault involving dozens of fighters. The facility initially under attack in Benghazi was separated by about a mile from a more-heavily staffed second facility — known as "the annex" — that hosted a CIA operation and other American personnel. No one had seen it coming — a British security team that returned some vehicles to the compound between 8:10 and 8:30 local time saw nothing out of the ordinary. With only seven U.S. staffers – five State Department security agents and their two protectees Smith and Stevens – at the scene of this first attack, it was easily overrun by the waves of hostile fighters. Ambassador Stevens – who'd concluded a meeting with a Turkish diplomat less than two hours before the gunshots – and Smith were shepherded by a security aide into a "safe room" in the compound.

But the attackers outside poured out cans of gasoline and set raging fires around two buildings, including their sanctuary, creating an intolerable inferno of heat and smoke. The security officer was unable to extract the two men from the building; Smith was later found by U.S. agents who got through in an armored vehicle, while Stevens was eventually taken to a hospital by Libyans but soon declared dead from smoke inhalation. The five security officers, and Sean Smith's body, were evacuated to the annex by members of the team stationed there.

And this was not the end of a bloody night in the eastern Libyan city. Shortly after 5 a.m. the next day – or 11 p.m., September 11, in Washington – there was a second wave of violence in Benghazi. This happened after a small group of CIA agents and other operatives arrived from the capital city of Tripoli to coordinate the evacuation of the Americans inside the annex. But new fighting erupted minutes after the rescuers arrived. Two skilled security personnel – Benghazi-based Tyrone S. Woods and Glen Doherty, who had just arrived from Tripoli – were both struck by mortar rounds on the rooftop of the annex as they tried to fight off the attackers and begin the evacuation.

Yet at the same time, something remarkable – stunning, really – had just happened. Even while the fighting in Benghazi was still underway, with CIA agents and State Department aides still taking enemy fire, a major-party candidate for president had issued a statement attacking the commander-in-chief's handling of the matter. Equally as shocking was that the statement was released during a day when both campaigns had supposedly disavowed negative campaigning as a small tribute to the nearly 3,000 Americans who'd been killed by terrorists on this date 11 years earlier.

After Obama, then-Secretary of State Hillary Clinton, and their colleagues had mourned the dead, and while the rubble was still being cleared from the compound, the secretary of state ordered an independent review of what happened in Benghazi headed by an Accountability Review Board, or ARB. For months, the panel performed the grim but necessary task of investigating any security lapses before the attacks, naming the officials who were involved, and making a lengthy list of recommendations to prevent a similar tragedy from happening in the future.

The heartbreaking night was also distinguished by incredible heroism. Lost in the grim news accounts about the deaths of the four diplomats and security aides was what a small group of Americans had accomplished in Benghazi — saving five U.S. personnel under heavy fire during the initial assault, recovering Smith's body at the height of the mayhem, and then evacuating roughly 30 people from the annex.

Hoax I: Mitt Romney's Statement

The Romney camp was very clear in explaining why it saw the tragic loss of life in Benghazi as an opportunity to go on the attack. "We've had this consistent critique and narrative on Obama's foreign policy," an anonymous Romney adviser said to *The New York Times*, "and we felt this was a situation that met our critique, that Obama really has been pretty weak in a number of ways on foreign policy, especially if you look at his dealings with the Arab Spring and its aftermath."[18] On the record, Romney advisor Lanhee Chen explained: "While there may be differences of opinion regarding issues of timing, I think everyone stands behind the critique of the administration, which we believe has conducted its foreign policy in a feckless manner."[19]

But outside the bubble of the Romney campaign, many political commentators viewed the late-night September 11 statement as a mistake both politically, morally, and factually. NBC's Chuck Todd called Romney's remarks "irresponsible" and "a bad mistake;" then-ABC correspondent Jake Tapper said it "does not stand up to simple chronology;" and *National Journal's* Ron Fournier described the Romney release as "ham-handed" and "inaccurate." Even conservative blogger and Fox News contributor Erick Erickson warned Romney to be "cautious."[20]

One of the biggest inaccuracies in the Romney statement was that in seeking to link the violence in Benghazi to the statement released by the Cairo embassy regarding *Innocence of Muslims*, the campaign ignored the central fact that the words came from an embassy led by a career diplomat which acted in the heat of a crisis without consulting the State Department, let alone the Obama inner circle. In fact, both the State Department and the White House had repudiated the statement – because its tone was too conciliatory – before the Romney statement had been released to the media.

Secretary of State Hillary Clinton quickly disowned the sentiment expressed by the embassy in a statement released at 10:08 p.m. ET, shortly before the Romney campaign issued its own missive. Clinton said, "The United States deplores any intentional effort to denigrate the religious beliefs of others. Our commitment to religious tolerance goes back to the very beginning of our nation. But let me be clear: There is never any justification for violent acts of this kind." Prior to the Romney campaign's condemnation, the White House had also washed its hands of the Cairo embassy's comments, telling *Politico* for a story published at 10:10 p.m. ET: "The statement by Embassy Cairo was not cleared by Washington and does not reflect the views of the United States government."[21]

Romney was clearly on the defensive when he addressed reporters in a hastily called news conference on September 12, as the final embers of the attack on the Benghazi compound were just dying out. At first, the GOP standard bearer did not exude confidence. "They clearly -- they clearly sent mixed messages to the world. And -- and the statement that came from the administration -- and the embassy is the administration -- the statement that came from the administration was a -- was a statement which is akin to apology and I think was a -- a -- a severe miscalculation," Romney said.[22]

Still, a political Rubicon had been crossed, and so the Republican nominee stuck by his overall message — even the parts that were demonstrably incorrect. "I also believe the administration was wrong to stand by a statement sympathizing with those who had breached our embassy in Egypt instead of condemning their actions," he said.

Romney's muddled message on the Middle East nonetheless quickly resonated with a right-wing media that has arisen largely to amplify messages from the GOP's leading politicians, not to analyze or fact-check them. In this case, the subliminal themes of the Benghazi hoax – that Obama somehow lacked American values and was prone to sympathizing with terrorists – had been an underpinning of right-wing discourse for more than three years. John Bolton, a leading neoconservative foreign policy official and Fox News contributor, told Fox host Greta Van Susteren that the incidents launched by extremists in Benghazi and Cairo were "in large measure caused by the weakness and fecklessness of the Obama administration's policies."[23]

These sentiments were reflected across Fox News. Appearing on *Special Report*, *Weekly Standard* senior writer Stephen Hayes acknowledged he wouldn't have held a press conference as Romney had, but nevertheless suggested that Benghazi amounted to a "partial collapse of the Obama doctrine: The leading-from-behind manifesto that has governed the way that the administration has conducted foreign policy over the past three-and-a-half years."[24]

Conservative pundit Ann Coulter, appearing on Sean Hannity's show, defended Romney by saying that his statement must have been "devastating to President Obama because the media is screaming bloody murder." Hannity replied, "I was actually thankful that we had a leader that actually came out and defended the United States of America and said that there will be consequences if you attack this country."[25]

Back in "the reality-based community," to borrow the phrase made famous by an unnamed adviser to George W. Bush in the mid-2000s, Obama and Clinton had already appeared together in the Rose Garden of the White House on September 12 to make exactly the kind of pledge that Hannity described. "The United States condemns in the strongest terms this outrageous and shocking attack," the president said. He added: "And make no mistake, we will work with the Libyan government to bring to justice the killers who attacked our people."[26]

It's hard to imagine a more forceful reaction, but conservative activists continued to push the day-one talking point that Obama's language and demeanor had somehow emboldened opponents of America. Lt.

Col. Anthony Shaffer, senior fellow at the Center for Advanced Defense Studies, a conservative think tank, told *Fox & Friends First* that deadly protests in Yemen over *Innocence of Muslims* were "a direct result of the milquetoast response of the president over the last 24 hours."[27]

Outside of the Fox News bubble, mainstream journalists, columnists, and editorial writers had a very different notion of who was being "feckless," to borrow that suddenly much-used term. Editorials blasted the Romney campaign for a "hyperbolic response," and for being "profoundly inappropriate." *The Des Moines Register* said Romney "should be ashamed"[28] while the *Pittsburgh Post-Gazette* questioned the candidate's "sensitivity, sense of decency and even his humanity."[29] *The Philadelphia Inquirer* summed up the consensus, writing that Romney "didn't wait for expert assessments ... to launch his own verbal assault."[30]

Even some conservatives jumped ship. Former Ronald Reagan speechwriter and *Wall Street Journal* columnist Peggy Noonan said on Fox News: "I don't feel that Mr. Romney has been doing himself any favors.... When hot things happen, cool words – or no words – is the way to go."[31] George W. Bush speechwriter and Daily Beast columnist David Frum wrote, "The Romney campaign's attempt to score political points on the killing of American diplomats was a dismal business in every respect."[32] Even Rep. Peter King (R-NY), chairman of the House Committee on Homeland Security and a stalwart Romney surrogate, said he "probably would have waited a day or half a day"[33] before publicly commenting.

It's not surprising that some of the more senior Republican heads would urge caution and moderation. After all, they'd seen outbreaks of violence against Americans and American interests in the Middle East dating back to the early 1970s – frustrating presidents and diplomats from both parties. Previous attacks had mostly produced a kind of rally-'round-the-flag effect – even when they occurred during the run-up to a presidential vote.

"An attack on any American is an attack on America," the GOP's 1996 White House nominee, Sen. Bob Dole, said that summer after a terrorist truck bombing on an American housing complex in Saudi Arabia called Khobar Towers killed 19 U.S. servicemen during the presidency of his opponent, Bill Clinton. "I would support whatever the Administration has in mind." Two years later, the eventual Republican nominee George W. Bush had a similar reaction when Clinton launched cruise missiles to retaliate for deadly attacks on two U.S. embassies in Africa. "I think you give the commander-in-chief the benefit of the doubt," said Bush, who would face Clinton's vice president, Al Gore, in 2000. "This is a foreign policy matter. I'm confident he's working on the best intelligence available, and I hope it's successful."[34]

It would be different with Benghazi – very different. A snap judgment made by a small circle of Romney advisers – in the heat of an already troubled campaign – to turn the unfolding crisis in Benghazi into a referendum on Obama's anti-terrorism policies had flipped the switch on a large, unwieldy ideological device. And once the right-wing noise machine was operating in full gear, and with all of its component pieces spinning in the halls of Congress, over the radio waves, and through fiber optic cables, it was all but impossible to shut off. When confronted with inconvenient truths about what really happened in Benghazi or how the government responded, the machine simply veered off in a new direction, or even made a 180-degree turn. What began as the Benghazi attack quickly morphed into the Benghazi hoax, made and manufactured by the American right.

Hoax II: Terrorism or an Act of Terror

One might think that Obama's solemn statement of September 12 strongly condemning the attack would have put to rest any questions about the president's resoluteness. But that's not how things worked in the right-wing media infrastructure. Instead of focusing on the clear message of Obama's remarks, right-wing commentators pored over and parsed words and diagrammed sentences, looking for signs of presidential weakness, on an audio frequency that only conservatives could hear.

Right-wing pundits honed in on two loosely related allegations. The first was that the White House had for too long conflated the *Innocence of Muslims* protests and the Benghazi attack even after the evidence showed there was little or no relationship. (This seemed an odd charge considering that the Romney campaign had done the same thing in its statement by immediately criticizing the State Department over comments made by embassy officials in Cairo, and news outlets such as *The New York Times* found witnesses in Benghazi who also believed a connection existed.[35]) The second charge was that Obama – either because of the confusion over the movie trailer protests, his alleged lack of passion or understanding of the terrorism fight, or raw political calculation – had used mealymouthed language that misled voters about the true import of Benghazi.

Sean Hannity laid out this allegation on Fox News, stating that members of the Obama administration "have culpability responsibility, they knew within 24 hours this was a terror attack. They knew this had nothing to do with the film. They knew that this was not spontaneous. But Susan Rice, Jay Carney, Hillary Clinton and the president himself, weeks later, they are still trying to sell their lie to the American people when they knew otherwise." He later added, "I think

17

this was all connected to the president not wanting to admit that they screwed up. And I think it's a cover-up."[36]

Elsewhere on the network, Romney foreign policy surrogate Bolton explained that Obama would be reluctant to call the attack terrorism because it undercut his ability to campaign on the death of Osama bin Laden: "[T]he war on terror is over. Al Qaeda's been defeated. Sweetness and light have broken out in Libya. That's what he thinks!"[37]

This tactic is nothing new; it, too, can be traced back to Obama's widely lauded June 2009 speech at American University in Cairo. As David Brock and I reported in our 2012 book *The Fox Effect*, following the speech, Fox News' managing editor, Bill Sammon, immediately sent an email to his staff claiming: "My cursory check of Obama's 6,000 word speech to the Muslim world did not turn up the words 'terror,' 'terrorist,' or 'terrorism.' "[38]

Ten minutes after sending the email, Sammon made that point on air on the network's dayside news program *America's Newsroom*. His argument was repeated on the network's programming at least three more times that day, and was featured on *Fox & Friends* the next morning.

But Fox's reporting was misleading: The president had devoted a lengthy section of the speech to the fight against Al Qaeda and "violent extremists who pose a grave threat to our security."[39] The message could not have been clearer – regardless of whether he used the actual word "terror."

Obama's semantic choices had a weird way of inflaming the right. Conservatives had created, in essence, a new type of political correctness. There was only one proper lexicon for discussing any type of attack or threat said to be inspired by Islam, regardless of its actual origin or scope. In the days immediately after the Al Qaeda attack on America on September 11, 2001, President Bush declared that America would wage a "global war on terror" – cast in the starkest moral terms, of the forces of good against an enemy that the 43rd president branded as "the evildoers." This new kind of "war" became so institutionalized that some eventually called it simply GWOT. Backed by a remarkably open-ended Authorization for Use of Military Force enacted by Congress in September 2001, it marked the first time that America had declared war not on a nation-state, but upon an ideology. The most enthusiastic backers of the GWOT described this as a war that could last for decades, possibly longer.

And so when President Obama was first elected in 2008, any discussion of terrorism connected to Islam that didn't use the Bush/ Cheney P.C.-for-conservatives lexicon — "terror," or "terrorist" — was instantly branded as proof of weakness, or worse. When his new administration unofficially stopped aggressively using the phrase "the global war on terror" and occasionally spoke of troops in Afghanistan or elsewhere as "overseas contingency operations," it drew ridicule from the likes of conservative writer David Limbaugh. He used the subtle change in tone to argue that the Obama administration was filled with "weak-willed leftists who are congenitally incapable of grasping the presence of evil in the world."[40]

Of course, Obama was simply doing what he'd promised the electoral majority that had supported him: not sounding like the third term of George W. Bush. After all, polls taken by organizations such as Pew and the BBC revealed American popularity declining steeply around the globe during the Bush 43 presidency, and one of Obama's main goals upon taking office in 2009 was to rebuild the U.S.'s sagging international alliances. His Cairo speech was a cornerstone of that effort. Ironically, despite the softer rhetoric at times, Obama arguably increased the scope and effectiveness of global anti-terrorism operations. In addition to the bin Laden mission, he sent a surge of new troops into Afghanistan and ordered drone strikes across several nations against Al Qaeda and its affiliates. But some activists and talking heads on the right were determined to pay attention not to what Obama did, but to what they thought they heard him say.

Dinesh D'Souza, the conservative pundit whose book and film *2016: Obama's America* were the rage in conservative circles during the summer and fall of 2012, promoted this purported weakness in the face of terrorism as a central theme of the president's philosophy, claiming that it indicated Barack Obama was "weirdly sympathetic to Muslim jihadis."[41]

The philosophy probably felt weird because it didn't really exist. But in the weeks following Benghazi, the smear that Obama had displayed an odd terrorist sympathy yet again started to cross over from the extreme right to more mainstream GOP discourse. Even Senate Minority Leader Mitch McConnell told Hannity: "You know the president had been out there claiming the war on terrorism was over. Bin Laden was dead. We're out of Iraq. We were getting out of Afghanistan. Everything was fine. And this terrorist attack killed four Americans, was inconvenient for them. It happened too soon, too close to the election and they wanted to act like it didn't happen."[42]

The crescendo of conservative criticism neared a peak as the second debate between Obama and Romney[43] – slated for October 16 at Hofstra University in New York – grew closer. The showdown would be in a town hall format, which meant that questions would come from members of the public and thus be less predictable than a mainstream-media-based affair. But Romney and his aides had clearly prepared for – and hoped for – a Benghazi question.

It came late in the debate. Audience member Kerry Ladka, a 61-year-old New Yorker, was called on by the moderator, CNN host Candy Crowley. He asked: "This question actually comes from a brain trust of my friends at Global Telecom Supply in Mineola yesterday. We were sitting around, talking about Libya, and we were reading and became aware of reports that the State Department refused extra security for our embassy in Benghazi, Libya, prior to the attacks that killed four

Americans. Who was it that denied enhanced security and why?"

After explaining what he had done to protect diplomats in the wake of the attack, the president used the opportunity to attack Romney, telling the audience, "While we were still dealing with our diplomats being threatened, Governor Romney put out a press release, trying to make political points, and that's not how a commander in chief operates. You don't turn national security into a political issue. Certainly not right when it's happening."

Romney responded by turning to the right's standard messaging on Obama: "The president's policies throughout the Middle East began with an apology tour and – and – and pursue a strategy of leading from behind, and this strategy is unraveling before our very eyes."

Crowley followed up with a question about Hillary Clinton's role in the attack. Barack Obama defended his secretary of state, saying, "Secretary Clinton has done an extraordinary job. But she works for me. I'm the president and I'm always responsible, and that's why nobody's more interested in finding out exactly what happened than I do. The day after the attack, governor, I stood in the Rose Garden and I told the American people and the world that we are going to find out exactly what happened. That this was an act of terror and I also said that we're going to hunt down those who committed this crime." Obama went on to call the accusation that his administration would play politics over Benghazi offensive.

Obama's comments sparked a heated back-and-forth that would have huge implications for the fall election. When it was his turn to respond, Romney rushed to attack the president over when he had finally termed the Benghazi attack "terrorism."

> "I think it's interesting the president just said something which – which is that on the day after the attack he went into the Rose Garden and said that this was an act of terror," said Romney in an

astonished voice.

"That's what I said," replied the president, slowly sipping a glass of water from his stool.

Pointing his finger at Obama and speaking as if he were a prosecutor about to finish off a witness, Romney went on: "You said in the Rose Garden the day after the attack, it was an act of terror. It was not a spontaneous demonstration, is that what you're saying?"

"Please proceed, governor," replied Obama calmly.

"I want to make sure we get that for the record," said Romney, turning to face the audience, "because it took the president 14 days before he called the attack in Benghazi an act of terror."

"Get the transcript," Obama responded.

As an astonished Romney turned to the moderator's table, Crowley said, "He did in fact, sir. So let me – let me call it an act of terror..."

Obama, clearly relishing the moment, shouted out, "Can you say that a little louder, Candy?"

"He did call it an act of terror," Crowley repeated to the shocked GOP candidate.[44]

With Crowley's utterance that Obama "did call it an act of terror," Romney's balloon was burst. It was a defining moment of the campaign, in more ways than one. In addition to squelching a minor Romney bounceback that had started with his respectable showing in the first debate in Denver, the exchange really captured the essence of the "Fox News effect" that takes place inside a corrosive conservative media bubble. Incredibly, Romney and his debate preparers had rehearsed an answer based upon what Fox News pundits were saying about the president's post-Benghazi statement – without taking the simple steps of learning what he'd actually said.

Here is more of Obama's September 12 statement: "No acts of terror will ever shake the resolve of this great nation, alter that character, or eclipse the light of the values that we stand for." The president continued: "Today we mourn four more Americans who represent the very best of the United States of America. We will not waver in our commitment to see that justice is done for this terrible act. And make no mistake, justice will be done."[45]

Romney and the right had also ignored congressional testimony from Obama administration official Matt Olsen, director of the National Counterterrorism Center. On September 19, in response to a question from then-Sen. Joe Lieberman, Olsen said that the victims in Benghazi "were killed in the course of a terrorist attack on our embassy."[46]

Administration officials had been looking at the possibility of a planned terrorist attack early on; so-called "open source" emails show that the State Department operations center was quickly made aware of a Sept. 11 Facebook posting purporting to be from the terror group Ansar al-Sharia claiming credit for the attack. But a second statement from Ansar al-Sharia on Sept. 12 denied responsibility – another sign of the conflicting early information the White House was sorting through.

Obama had never sought to declare an early end to America's stepped-up operations against terrorism, even though some pundits had urged him to do exactly that. Conservatives claimed that Obama didn't want to discuss "terror" because he wanted to fool voters into thinking Al Qaeda had been vanquished. Yet at the president's acceptance speech at the Democratic convention in Charlotte several days before the Benghazi attack, he said: "[F]or all the progress we've made, challenges remain. Terrorist plots must be disrupted."[47]

Months later, long after the debate flap with Romney, Obama told reporters he was dumbstruck over what exactly he was supposed to be covering up. "Who executes some sort of cover-up or effort to tamp things down for three days?" the commander-in-chief wondered.[48]

That was a good question. At this point, one might have expected that the Republican noise machine would have turned down the volume on Benghazi. After all, the first two attempts to make political hay out of an attack that killed four Americans had – not surprisingly – crashed and burned in spectacular fashion. After the first Romney statement had been widely condemned as unseemly, the debate smackdown assisted by moderator Crowley had robbed the Republican candidate of his first-debate momentum.

But what happened in Benghazi had clearly struck an emotional nerve for the far right that became unmoored from facts. Too many right-wing pundits, and the rank-and-file "dittoheads" who follow their marching orders, still felt that a narrative would emerge from Libya that would show that Obama did not understand their "global war on terror," that he actually sympathized with terrorists and felt little or nothing over the loss of American life. And if that narrative did not emerge organically, they would craft it themselves.

Indeed, the new effort to sow doubt about Obama's resoluteness began just minutes after the Hofstra debate ended. During a post-debate interview with Romney surrogate Sununu, Fox host Bret Baier chimed in and insisted that Obama meant his Rose Garden reference to terror "generically" rather than "specifically speaking about Benghazi."[49]

In the truly remarkable 48-hour span that followed the debate, Fox would air a total of 55 segments, comprising four hours of airtime, to attempt to explain away Barack Obama's use of the phrase "acts of terror."[50] *Fox News Sunday* host Chris Wallace would air a deceptively edited video of Obama's Rose Garden address, removing critical context from the statement; correspondent John Roberts would call it "unclear" whether Obama had been talking about Benghazi when he referenced "acts of terror" during that segment; and the network's Steve Centanni would ignore subsequent comments to suggest that the Rose Garden comments were an outlier.[51] [52] [53] But their efforts were clearly making no headway with the dwindling number of undecided voters. For a brief moment, Benghazi faded as Republicans searched in vain for another trumped-up scandal, hoping to catch lightning in a bottle as Election Day neared. Meanwhile, throughout the political season, the independent ARB panel that Secretary of State Clinton had convened in mid-September was painstakingly interviewing witnesses in Libya and in Washington, conducting the real business of identifying security failures with virtually no coverage in the mainstream press.

President Obama's solid re-election victory over Romney on November 6, 2012, did not squash the bogus notion that the White House had used weasel words about what had happened in Benghazi. Six months later in May, for example, House Committee on Oversight and Government Reform Chairman Darrell Issa, who was leading the Benghazi investigation, was asked by Fox host Megyn Kelly about the administration's supposed Benghazi cover-up. Issa told the host, "Act of terror is different than a terrorist attack. The truth is, [Benghazi] was a terrorist attack, this had Al Qaeda at it."[54]

It was almost comical, this notion that an "act of terror" was somehow substantively different than "a terrorist attack." Such linguistic contortions should have made it clear that Republicans' real issue was not with the words but with the mouth they were coming out of – that practically no pronouncement from a Democrat named Barack Hussein Obama, with that exotic name and equally exotic background, would sound aggressive enough for them.

Still, some on the far right could not let go of their muddled thinking on Benghazi – and when a new opportunity arose shortly after Election Day, they pounced.

Hoax III: The Attack on Susan Rice

Not long after the election, a front-runner emerged to replace Hillary Clinton as secretary of state: U.N. Ambassador Susan Rice. Rice certainly had the right credentials — a former Rhodes Scholar who'd served as assistant secretary of state for African affairs under President Bill Clinton and a top adviser to 2004 Democratic candidate John Kerry. And she had the one intangible quality that is most important for the job of America's top diplomat: The complete trust and confidence of President Obama. But there was one obstacle in her way. Several top Republicans had already threatened to go to extraordinary lengths to block her confirmation. The reason: her bit part — albeit a highly controversial one — in the Benghazi affair.

It started on September 16, 2012, just five days after the attack, when the death of the U.S. ambassador and the three others was still a front-burner news story. The major networks reached out to the Obama White House for a guest who could represent the administration on the Sunday morning talk shows, and Rice was given the task.

Rice appeared on five channels that day — ABC, NBC, CBS, Fox, and CNN. Her message derived largely from talking points that had been prepared for the House Permanent Select Committee on Intelligence and distributed to her in advance of the interviews. Rice was clear on two things: First, her knowledge was drawn from the intelligence community's currently available information, but in the midst of an ongoing investigation, its understanding could change. And second, it was the assessment of the intelligence community at the time that the attacks were inspired by the anti-Islam video posted on YouTube that had inspired protests, some violent, in more than 20 countries in the Arab world.

She told Jake Tapper of ABC News, "[T]here's an FBI investigation that has begun and will take some time to be completed." Additionally, she said, the attack was "spontaneous – not a premeditated – response to what had transpired in Cairo." She concluded, "We'll wait to see exactly what the investigation finally confirms, but that's the best information we have at present." Her responses in the other interviews were similar.[55]

With each passing day, evidence emerged that strengthened the case that this was a planned and well-coordinated attack, and most likely not violence that had emerged organically from a protest over the *Innocence of Muslims* movie. In fact, there were conflicting reports over whether any protest had taken place outside the Benghazi compound, or whether the streets were empty before the gunfire began. When a clear consensus emerged, signified by the September 19 Senate testimony of administration official Matt Olsen, that the attack was planned and connected to known terrorist groups, conservatives began to ask the same questions about Rice they had initially raised about President Obama. Had there been a deliberate attempt to mislead, with the goal of convincing voters there was no more Al Qaeda threat?

"She goes out, she's the one who says, this is all just the video," said former Bush Press Secretary turned Fox host Dana Perino on September 21, five days after Rice's interviews. "Three days later, we find out that that is completely wrong. How does that happen?"

"Honestly, Dana, it looks and smells and probably is a cover-up," replied co-host Eric Bolling. He added that the "White House is covering up for what is going to end up being a terrorist attack on American soil" for political reasons.[56]

Indeed, conservatives attacked Rice by implicating her in a deliberate cover-up of the nature of the attacks several times during the run-up to the November election, but they never gained much traction, particularly after Romney had been humiliated in trying to make an issue of Benghazi at the October 16 debate. However, the attacks on Rice abruptly resumed almost as soon as the presidential votes were counted. Targeting Rice and her rumored nomination as secretary of state was Political Strategy 101: a chance for Republican senators to score points on Obama and change the conversation after Romney's defeat. It was also an opportunity to revive Benghazi as an issue generally and wipe away some of the embarrassment caused by the initial backfiring of the GOP's conspiracy theories.

In December, Republican Sens. Lindsey Graham, John McCain, and Kelly Ayotte, all hawkish, neoconservative lawmakers who regularly push for military action against countries in the Middle East, would publicly declare Rice unfit to serve as secretary of state. The reason was her Sunday show appearances about Benghazi.

South Carolina's Graham went first, announcing somewhat cryptically: "Somebody has got to start paying a price around this place." Added Graham: "I am dead-set on making sure we don't promote anybody that was an essential player in the Benghazi debacle." Rather than rally around the American flag in a unified response to an unprovoked attack, the Beltway GOP was still looking for a scapegoat, even after the election – and their rhetoric was starting to lose all proportionality. Graham was attempting, in essence, to put blood on Susan Rice's hands, concluding, "This is about the role she played around four dead Americans."[57]

McCain attacked Rice during an appearance on CNN, claiming that "everybody knew that it was an Al Qaeda attack, and she continued to tell the world through all of the talk shows that it was a 'spontaneous demonstration' sparked by a video."[58] On Fox News that day, McCain announced: "I will do everything in my power to block her from being the United States secretary of state."[59]

In a sad way, the verbal broadsides against Rice continued a pattern that had started during Obama's first term. Just as conservative commentators continually charged that the first black president on some level fundamentally didn't understand America, the most fervent criticism of Obama aides seemed focused on African-Americans, including the controversial Attorney General Eric Holder, green jobs adviser Van Jones, who was forced out of office, and now Rice.

Her attempts to meet with senators and mollify their concerns only seemed to make the situation worse. Lindsay Graham announced following their meeting, "The concerns I have today are greater than they were before."[60] Even Republican Maine Sen. Susan Collins, arguably the most moderate senator in the caucus, was buying in, telling CNN: "It's important that the secretary of state enjoy credibility around the world with Congress and here in our country as well. And I am concerned that Susan Rice's credibility may have been damaged by the misinformation that was presented that day."[61]

On December 13, Rice bowed to reality and officially withdrew her name from consideration for the post at State. A short time later, Massachusetts Sen. John Kerry was nominated to replace Clinton as secretary of state, while Rice became Obama's national security adviser, a critical post that does not require Senate confirmation. Still, Rice's problems up on Capitol Hill were mindboggling. Her official functions had nothing to do with the diplomatic facilities in Benghazi. As U.N. ambassador, Rice had no operational ties with either the personnel on the ground from either the State Department or the CIA. She was simply acting as an administration spokeswoman. Incredibly, her potential nomination collapsed not because she'd done anything wrong, but because experienced Republican senators had embraced a cooked-up cable TV scandal.

It's important to remember that two major news organizations — including one that had a reporter on the ground on the night of September 11 — were still reporting long after Rice's TV appearances that they had interviewed Libyan eyewitnesses who insisted there was at least some connection between the anti-Muslim film and the assault.

Here is what *The New York Times* – which had a journalist in Benghazi – reported in October, a full month after Rice's appearances:

> To Libyans who witnessed the assault and know the attackers, there is little doubt what occurred: a well-known group of local Islamist militants struck the United States Mission without any warning or protest, and they did it in retaliation for the video. That is what the fighters said at the time, speaking emotionally of their anger at the video without mentioning Al Qaeda, Osama bin Laden or the terrorist strikes of 11 years earlier. And it is an explanation that tracks with their history as members of a local militant group determined to protect Libya from Western influence.[62]

Also in October 2012, the Huffington Post reported, "On Sept. 12, Reuters reported that there were protesters present when the U.S. consulate in Benghazi was attacked and described the assailants as 'part of a mob blaming America for a film they said insulted the Prophet Mohammad.'" Reuters correspondent Hadeel Al-Shalchi told the website that "she reported what people 'told me they saw that day,' all of whom she met face to face."[63]

In other words, if two of the world's most respected newsrooms with journalists reporting from Benghazi were still insisting weeks after the attack that there appeared to be a connection to *Innocence of Muslims*, was what Rice said just five days afterward really a career-altering error? The failure to resolve whether or not there had been a riot and whether the video had anything to do with it would be an enduring part of the Benghazi conversation – one not fully resolved to this day.

But more importantly, Rice was given talking points on the Benghazi attack prior to her Sunday show interviews that had been drafted and approved by the intelligence community. This was not unusual – when an administration official appears in the media, they are typically provided with talking points. These points are especially crucial when related to national security to ensure that classified information is not accidentally disclosed.

The talking points Rice received stated the attacks in Benghazi "were spontaneously inspired by the protests at the U.S. Embassy in Cairo." The Cairo protests had been directly linked to the YouTube video in question, hence it was not out of bounds for Rice to draw a connection between the two, the core of the conservative complaint.[64]

Later, as even more information emerged about the talking points prepared by the intelligence agencies, the Huffington Post asked John McCain if he should apologize to Susan Rice for dragging her name through the mud. He responded, "No, of course not."[65] Lindsay Graham went even further, telling Fox News: "[A]s to Susan Rice, she's not going to get an apology from me. She's going to get a subpoena."[66]

Rice's decision not to seek the State Department posting, while understandable and probably unavoidable because of the unified Republican opposition, no matter how unfounded, meant that right-wing pundits and their political enablers now smelled blood in the water over Benghazi. If the incomplete information given by Rice on the talk shows was truly the result of these talking points, then, they convinced each other, the talking points themselves were central to the Obama administration cover-up that they were positive had taken place.

Indeed, as we saw in the months that would follow, the issue of the talking points that Rice consulted – who wrote them, what was their purpose – would rise and fall several times, raised at congressional hearings or in news accounts, only to be shot down again and again. At times it felt as if the Republicans and their allies in the punditocracy were using some kind of scandal Twister wheel, spinning it again and again to see who or what would come up this month – Obama, Secretary of State Clinton, the ARB panel, the military response or the testimony of so-called "whistleblowers." The story of the talking points is especially illustrative.

Hoax IV: The Talking Points

Of all the figures connected to the Obama administration, no one would seem less likely to be the target of a Republican witch hunt than the former CIA director, David Petraeus. He was the leading general behind the "surge" in troop presence that contributed to the stabilization of Iraq after more than three years of fighting, later the top U.S. general in Afghanistan, and a leading authority on counterterrorism. Petraeus was idolized in conservative circles. Many on the right had hoped he would enter politics and seek the Republican nomination for president someday. When Petraeus retired from the Army to join the Obama administration as CIA director in September 2011, the move was one more development that undercut the conservative argument that the president was weak or even sympathetic to terrorists.

The talking points that Susan Rice used on the September 16 talk shows originated with Petraeus. Three days after the attack in Benghazi, he sat down with members of the House Permanent Select Committee on Intelligence, or HPSCI. Petraeus shared classified details about the attack on the American compound. Recognizing that attendees in the meeting were likely to be questioned by reporters about the attacks, C.A. "Dutch" Ruppersberger (D-MD), ranking member of the House Intelligence Committee, wanted to ensure that members of Congress did not reveal classified information and asked Petraeus to have the CIA generate talking points that they could use in public. "We didn't want to jeopardize sources and methods," the congressman later told *The Washington Post*, "and we didn't want to tip off the bad guys."[67]

Following the meeting with Ruppersberger, an email with the subject line "FLASH coordination — white paper for HPSCI" was sent to the various agencies coordinating the response to the Benghazi attacks, informing recipients of the need for "unclassified points immediately that [members of Congress] can use in talking to the media."[68]

Over the next 24 hours, a set of talking points was drafted by the CIA's Office of Terrorism Analysis, and then altered multiple times through an interagency process involving the State Department, the White House, and others. In the end, much of the intelligence agency's specifics about the suspected perpetrators of the attack were removed in order to preserve the criminal investigation. The result was a set of talking points that stated:

- The currently available information suggests that the demonstrations in Benghazi were spontaneously inspired by the protests at the US Embassy in Cairo and evolved into a direct assault against the US diplomatic post in Benghazi and subsequently its annex. There are indications that extremists participated in the violent demonstrations.

- This assessment may change as additional information is collected and analyzed and as currently available information continues to be evaluated.

- The investigation is on-going, and the US Government is working with Libyan authorities to bring to justice those responsible for the deaths of US citizens.[69]

The release of the talking points clearly shows that Rice closely followed the information that she had been given. But it does raise legitimate questions about why the document includes information linking the attack to the Cairo protests over the YouTube video, if government agents knew early on that the attack was planned and coordinated in Benghazi. To conservative opponents of the president, only one theory made sense – that the White House had somehow doctored the talking points to divert attention from the role of organized Islamist extremists, for political purposes.

John McCain pointed the finger right at the White House. "I think it's patently obvious that the talking points that Ambassador Rice had didn't come from the CIA. It came from the White House," he told Fox's Greta Van Susteren. "So who in the White House gave Ambassador Rice those, quote, 'talking points' that she used, when clearly, the facts had contradicted that kind of assertion to the American people?" According to McCain, while Rice had blamed a "hateful video," it was clearly an "Al Qaeda operation." And not only was the Arizona senator convinced that he knew what had happened, but he insisted that he knew why: "it interferes with the president's narrative, 'we got bin Laden, Al Qaeda's on the run, therefore I'm a great commander in chief.' "[70]

And yet the talking points had emerged in consultation with Petraeus, a man that McCain had called "one of the greatest generals in American history."[71] In November 16 congressional testimony, Petraeus – by then the former CIA chief – testified that he had signed off on the talking points before they were distributed.[72] Petraeus would have had little to gain from misleading Congress, given both his track record of political independence and the enormous respect that he had from members of both parties. Just days before he testified, Petraeus had been forced out of the CIA by the revelation of an extramarital affair – but that matter also had seemingly no bearing on his ability to tell the truth about Benghazi.

Petraeus acknowledged that classified intelligence at the time had indicated that the attack had been committed by terrorists. But according to Petraeus, details about the perpetrators, including the intelligence community's belief that members of an Al Qaeda-linked group had participated, were removed from the public explanation of the attack not for political reasons, but in order to prevent the terrorists from learning that American intelligence and law enforcement agencies were pursuing them and thus preserve the criminal investigation.[73]

It would later be revealed that the initial draft of talking points authored by the CIA had said that the attacks in Benghazi "were spontaneously inspired by the protests at the US Embassy in Cairo" – a reference to the protests (and thus the video that triggered them) that predated any editing by other administration officials. Indeed, the White House would eventually take the unprecedented step, in May 2013, of publicly releasing more than 100 pages of internal emails about the talking points, in order to clear up any lingering doubts. They provided proof that the intelligence community, not the White House, had been the first to link the attacks with the video, debunking conservative claims that the connection had been dreamed up by the administration for political reasons.[74]

Before the end of 2012, some knowledgeable military analysts were already tiring of the Benghazi hoax. In late November, longtime Pentagon expert and author Thomas Ricks appeared on Fox News and stunned interviewer Jon Scott by dismissing any alleged scandal as hype and questioning why the network hadn't focused this much on scores of contractor deaths in Iraq. "So when I see this focus on what was essentially a small firefight, I think, number one, I've covered a lot of firefights. It's impossible to figure out what happens in them sometimes," Ricks continued. "And second, I think that the emphasis on Benghazi has been extremely political, partly because Fox was operating as a wing of Republican Party."

Fox News' Scott was stunned and instantly ended the interview. "All right. Tom Ricks, thanks very much for joining us today."[75]

It was highly revealing – and yet a brief setback for Fox News and the other scandalmongers. The arrival of a new Congress in January gave their scheme new life.

Hoax V: The Republican Investigations

Since the Bill Clinton presidency in the 1990s, congressional investigations have been a leading arm of the Republican noise machine.
When the GOP took control of Congress two years into the Obama
administration, Republicans seized control of key investigatory panels
with the full intent of using their powers to bludgeon the White House
– just as they'd done with Clinton after their party's sweep in 1994.
Famously, then-Rep. Dan Burton (R-IN) used his time in the late
1990s as chair of the House Committee on Oversight and Government
Reform to mount lengthy and mostly fruitless investigations, such as
one into Democratic Party fundraising that the *Washington Post* editorial
page described as verging on "its own cartoon, a joke, and a deserved
embarrassment."[76]

Now, with President Obama transitioning to his second term, the
GOP was back behind the wheel of its big scandal machine – yet still
searching for a scandal after two years. Leading the charge were two
House Republicans, Darrell Issa of California, the chairman of the
Committee on Oversight and Government Reform, and Jason Chaffetz,
a Tea Party member from Utah and the chairman of that committee's
Subcommittee on National Security. From these perches, they would
lead both the investigations of Benghazi and efforts to spin the scandal
in the press.

Issa is one of the wealthiest members of Congress, parlaying a
successful car alarm company into multiple political campaigns,
including a failed run for Senate in 1998 in which he spent $10 million
of his personal fortune only to lose the Republican primary.[77] After a
decade in the House of Representatives, he rose to become chairman of
the Oversight Committee, a posting that not only increased his power
in the chamber but his prominence in the national media as well. To

advance his political career to new heights, Issa would need to develop scandal storylines that editors would deem juicy enough for the front page.

Shortly before the 2010 congressional elections and the GOP takeover, Issa drew flak for telling Rush Limbaugh that Obama was "one of the most corrupt presidents in modern times." (He later walked that statement back.)[78]

Utah's Chaffetz – Issa's investigative-minded colleague – is a three-term congressman who has moved steadily to the right over his political lifetime. The former placekicker for Brigham Young University's football team was actually a state co-chairman for Democrat Michael Dukakis in 1988 (perhaps because his dad had been Kitty Dukakis' first husband before they divorced and she remarried the Massachusetts politician).[79] He later worked for Utah's moderate GOP Gov. Jon Huntsman as a campaigner and chief of staff. But once in Congress, he quickly became a conservative star and a regular presence on the programs of far-right media figures such as Glenn Beck. In the wake of the Benghazi attacks, Chaffetz worked harder than any Republican in Congress to make the issue his own, traveling to Libya and appearing as a spokesman on television almost as much as Issa, his senior on the Oversight panel.

House committees such as Issa's play a critical role because despite the checkered history of the 1990s the mainstream media continue to view these bodies as authoritative sources that bring credibility to an issue as an arm of Congress. In reality, these GOP-driven House investigations have become maddeningly successful conduits for deceptively framed snippets of transcript from congressional interviews and cherry-picked administration documents.

Conservative media have praised the Republican investigations for their alleged nonpartisanship. "[A]nyone who says this is politically driven, or it's against the president, that's out the window," said *Fox & Friends* co-host Brian Kilmeade during a May 6 segment. "Because if there's a non-political season in this world in American politics, it's now" – a patently ludicrous claim in a springtime of heated debates over everything from immigration to gun violence to funding health care reform.[80]

Indeed, the GOP-led hearings kept coming in waves even as some leading Republicans acknowledged they had sufficient facts on Benghazi. "I feel like I know what happened in Benghazi. I'm fairly satisfied," Tennessee Sen. Bob Corker said on MSNBC's *The Daily Rundown* in May 2013. "But look, the House wants to have hearings, I hope they're done in a respectful way and hopefully it will shed some light on what happened."[81]

Led by Issa and Chaffetz, the seemingly endless House investigation into the Benghazi terrorist attacks has been marred by embarrassments, factual errors, and "accidental" disclosures of classified material. Despite three hearings, dozens of leaks, and scores of interviews, in addition to the receipt of at least 25,000 of pages of documents, the committee has failed to produce any information that could lay blame on President Obama, Hillary Clinton, or any of its other targets for what took place the night of September 11, 2012, or during the administration's response. It has stood in stark contrast to the professionalism of the independent ARB probe, and the Obama administration's efforts to implement its recommendations over the course of 2013. In spite of that, the administration has repeatedly cooperated in every possible way with this seemingly unending labyrinth of probes up on Capitol Hill.

The investigatory arm seeking facts to prove conservatives' bizarre insistence that President Obama is "weirdly sympathetic" to terrorists had a knack for making public information that might someday prove helpful to terrorists. While discussing the security force that helped rescue those in the compound, Republican members outed the fact that Benghazi had housed a sizable CIA operation, something that until that point had not been confirmed to the public.

At one of the first hearings in early October 2012, State Department officials went before Issa's committee to discuss the security lapses at the diplomatic compound, and Chaffetz accidentally revealed classified details about the compound when a State Department official, in order to explain the events of September 11, 2012, used publicly available satellite imagery. Chaffetz loudly objected: "I was told specifically while I was in Libya I could not and should not ever talk about what you're showing here today."[82]

With that outburst, Chaffetz revealed that something in the photo itself was classified – a fact that would not have been known had he not spoken up. Issa had the visual display removed, though C-SPAN's audience could simply rewind its DVRs if it wanted to take another look.

Chaffetz cavalierly defended himself later, telling The Huffington Post, "It's borne itself out that, yeah, that was classified, and they shouldn't have raised it."[83] For Chaffetz, there was no shame in making such an error. Instead, Benghazi became a coming-out party for the Utah representative, parlaying the issue into dozens of appearances on Fox as he loudly echoed the network's accusations of a cover-up in Benghazi. It was very good politics – feeding the Fox News machine had boosted the likes of Rep. Michele Bachmann (R-MN) from obscure back-bencher to 2012 presidential candidate, after all. But it had very little to do with finding the truth.

Nine days later, Issa's committee made public more than 150 pages of State Department documents and communications related to the attacks at the compound. But the committee failed to redact the names of Libyan civilians and officials working with Americans from those documents, thereby putting their lives in danger. An administration source told Foreign Policy magazine's Josh Rogin, "This does damage to the individuals because they are named, danger to security cooperation because these are militias and groups that we work with and that is now well known, and danger to the investigation, because these people could help us down the road."[84] The cables exposed a female human rights advocate fighting against violence, a port manager working with the

U.S., and "a local militia commander dishing dirt on the inner workings of the Libyan Interior Ministry,"[85] among others.

These revelations put the lives of sources on the ground helping the U.S. government in real danger, yet Issa and Chaffetz showed no concern. They believed their political agenda took precedence. "Anything below 'Secret' is in fact just a name on a piece of paper," Issa said at a meeting with State Department officials. "And I think it is important to understand that. So if you have seen papers that say 'for official use only,' 'State Department sensitive,' that is crap."[86]

There was another great irony about the House probe. A large reason that a congressional investigation has received credence in the mainstream media is the bipartisan makeup of the committee – yet minority-party opinions have not been welcome as part of Issa's probe. An October 2012 memo from minority committee staff to Democratic members made clear the extent to which they were locked out of the process. "Although Chairman Issa has claimed publicly that 'we are pursuing this on a bipartisan basis,' the Committee's investigation into the attack in Benghazi has been extremely partisan," wrote the staff.[87] "The Chairman and his staff failed to consult with Democratic Members prior to issuing public letters with unverified allegations, concealed witnesses and refused to make one hearing witness available to Democratic staff, withheld documents obtained by the Committee during the investigation, and effectively excluded Democratic Committee Members from joining a poorly-planned congressional delegation to Libya."

"This is investigation by press release and does a disservice to our common goal of ensuring that our diplomatic corps serving overseas has the best protection possible to do its critical work," House Oversight Committee ranking member Elijah Cummings (D-MD) said in a statement released to coincide with another hearing in May 2013.[88] Instead, any so-called "finding" by these Republican-led probes has had a strictly political bent.

Indeed, the breathlessly partisan nature of the probe is not just a powerful indictment of the Benghazi hoax, but a sad commentary on how far Republicans had drifted in just a couple of generations from what were once truly bipartisan congressional investigations. In the Watergate era, it was a Republican senator – Howard Baker of Tennessee – who famously asked what did a Republican president know, and when did he know it.

Hoax VI: The Fake Concussion

One of the reasons that Republicans were so eager to push their Benghazi investigation was the chance to summon the outgoing secretary of state, Hillary Clinton, before Congress and grill her in public about what the State Department knew before, during, and after the attack on its compound. Requesting her testimony did not seem unreasonable: Clinton could offer insights about what America's highest-ranking diplomats knew about the situation in Libya; in an ideal world, those observations might aid the ostensible goal of a forward-looking investigation, to strengthen security procedures at U.S. diplomatic posts. But Clinton was a high-value political target for Republicans, due to the widely discussed possibility she would enter the 2016 presidential race as an instant front-runner. Staged questions on Capitol Hill could theoretically tarnish her resume, her reputation, and her chances.

Clinton was looking to appear before the panel before Christmas of 2012 – and then real life interfered. On December 15, *The Washington Post* reported that, according to a State Department spokesperson, Clinton had suffered a concussion after being ill with a stomach virus, becoming dehydrated, and fainting. Due to her condition, Clinton canceled an appearance before the Senate Foreign Relations Committee to discuss Benghazi.

The reaction to this news was extraordinary. Journalists are trained to be highly skeptical – there's a famous saying: "If your mother says she loves you, check it out!" But on conservative news outlets – especially, of course, Fox News – reporters and commentators practically raced into the studio to relate their completely unsourced and unfounded suspicions that Clinton was not at all ill, but merely wished to avoid the hot lights of the hearing room. It was as if these opinion journalists had been broadcasting their gut feeling that Benghazi was a cover-up for so long that they had now lost any inner voice telling them to first gather more information to confirm what had actually happened to the secretary of state.

Fox News' Megyn Kelly and Monica Crowley first raised the issue during the December 17 edition of Kelly's daytime news program, *America Live*. Kelly asked Crowley, "What's really going on? I mean, she fainted sometime last week and can't show up this Thursday for a previously scheduled testimony? I mean, there was speculation, I want all the viewers to know, about whether she'd really go" to the Benghazi hearing even before her illness. Kelly then said, "I'm not suggesting she didn't get a concussion. But there is a legitimate question about, is – do we believe this is an excuse and that she really will show up to testify?" Crowley responded by referring to Clinton's illness as "this virus with apparently impeccable timing."

Now Fox and its allies in the right-wing media were off and running. Later that night, John Bolton, the former U.N. ambassador, claimed that Hillary was suffering from "a diplomatic illness" that he said befalls foreign-service officers when they "don't want to go to a meeting or conference or event."[89]

Three days later, almost every prime-time Fox News program had spread innuendo about Hillary Clinton's health.

The four conservative hosts of *The Five* suggested that Clinton's illness had been faked to avoid testifying on Benghazi. Greg Gutfeld asked if it was "offensive to question the odd timing of an illness," because those making the accusations were simply "exercising our First Amendment right to ask questions." His co-host Andrea Tantaros accused Hillary of "being a professional victim."[90]

On Fox's flagship news program, *Special Report*, Charles Krauthammer claimed Clinton was "suffering from acute Benghazi allergy which causes lightheadedness when she hears the word 'Benghazi'"[91] – an assessment he repeated when appearing with Sean Hannity.

Fox wasn't the only outlet to question Clinton's health. The *New York Post* headlined its doubtful reporting: "Hillary Clinton's head fake."[92] And the *Los Angeles Times* mainstreamed the concussion accusation with a reader poll asking, "Did she fake it?"[93]

State Department spokesperson Victoria Nuland told reporters that those casting aspersions on Clinton's health "are people who don't know what they're talking about." She also said, "It's really unfortunate that in times like this people make wild speculation based on no information."[94] In fact, Clinton had suffered a serious concussion – so serious that she would be admitted to the hospital later that month with a blood clot resulting from the injury.[95] Hillary Clinton's doctors released a statement announcing that the secretary of state experienced a blood clot "between the brain and the skull behind the right ear" and stating that she was being treated with blood thinners to prevent any lasting brain damage.

In late January after she had recovered, Clinton appeared before two congressional committees to discuss Benghazi. It was never in doubt that the outgoing secretary of state would testify before the committee – it was simply a question of timing.

Some Republicans even felt their ideological colleagues had gone too far. A GOP consultant and a former spokesman for Texas Sen. Kay Bailey Hutchison named Matt Mackowiak posted on Twitter: "Some of us had some fun w/ Hillary's concussion & postponing of Hill testimony. Clearly a serious situation. Apologies & prayers in order."[96]

Indeed, but apologies like Mackowiak's were rare. For the second time in less than four months, Republicans had been not just wrong on Benghazi, but embarrassed to the point of humiliation – the point where one might expect these partisans to walk away, perhaps in search of new issues. But to expect that would be to misunderstand the nature of the modern Republican noise machine and what groupthink like the Benghazi hoax means to its various cogs. After all, on issues of great national importance like climate change — where the world's top climatologists have presented repeated proof that manmade greenhouse gases pose perilous consequences for the planet — conservatives have repeatedly cocooned into their bubble of self-dealing experts and think-tank-invented rebuttals. Retreat is never an option, and the Benghazi hoax would be no different. The official start of the new Obama term would instead create multiple spinoffs of the hoax — each one a dead end.

Hoax VII: Hillary Clinton Faked Her Emotion

When Hillary Clinton finally did appear before the State Department's House and Senate committees of jurisdiction in January, the notion that the outgoing secretary of state wanted to duck testifying seemed a tad silly. In contrast to the Republicans' conspiracy theories, Clinton's testimony grounded what had happened on September 11, 2012, back in reality — reminding people that Benghazi was viewed by those in the State Department and the administration not as a time of political calculation but a moment of anguish over losing friends and co-workers.

"For me, this is not just a matter of policy, it's personal. I stood next to President Obama as the Marines carried those flag-draped caskets off the plane at Andrews." Clinton said, tearing up as she spoke before the Senate Foreign Relations Committee. "I put my arms around the mothers and fathers, the sisters and brothers, the sons and daughters, and the wives left alone to raise their children." A diplomatic security officer severely injured in the attack was still recovering at Walter Reed National Military Medical Center at the time she was testifying.[97]

But that was not why the senators had called her to Capitol Hill. As the hearing dragged on, Clinton became openly irritated with Republicans' continued focus on ephemera — particularly the talking points Ambassador Susan Rice had used during her appearances on the Sunday shows five days after the attacks and the question of whether the attack was premeditated or a reaction to the anti-Muslim film.

"With all due respect, the fact is we had four dead Americans," Clinton told Wisconsin Republican Senator Ron Johnson, her voice rising with passion. "Was it because of a protest? Or was it because of guys out for a walk one night who decided that they would go kill some Americans? What difference at this point does it make?"

She then pivoted to the heart of the matter: "It is our job to figure out what happened and do everything we can to prevent it from ever happening again, Senator."[98]

In that one heated hearing-room moment, Clinton gave voice not just to her own frustration but to that of regular citizens who were utterly baffled as to why this American tragedy overseas – the kind of event that once united and galvanized leaders of both parties and the public – was instead being used in a largely unsuccessful effort to score cheap political points, not once, but again and again and again. Why were Republicans so focused on talking points used on Sunday shows watched by a small fraction of the U.S. population? Why was this being described as the greatest cover-up since Watergate – a scandal involving repeated break-ins, bugging, and massive misuse of the FBI, CIA, and other federal agencies?

Hillary Clinton had finally had enough. The same could not be said of conservatives. They were just getting started.

Even as Clinton's tears had not yet dried, Fox contributor Laura Ingraham used her Twitter account to accuse her of "lip-synching crying about Benghazi victims"[99] during the hearings. Rush Limbaugh called it "part of the script."[100]

Senator Johnson also complained that Clinton had faked her reaction during their particularly heated exchange on the subject. Speaking with BuzzFeed, he said: "I think she just decided before she was going to describe emotionally the four dead Americans, the heroes, and use that as her trump card to get out of the questions."[101] Sean Hannity would chime in that the incident was "staged, probably at the direction of" Democratic strategist James Carville.[102]

It was almost laughable. If Clinton's testimony had been delivered in flat, unemotional tones or had downplayed the death of the Americans, you can be certain that conservatives would have jumped all over that, accusing her of lack of empathy for those fighting terrorism.

Instead, in making light of her display of emotion, they were walking down a familiar path, one that bordered on sexism. While seeking the presidency in 2008, Clinton's voice broke while answering audience questions in New Hampshire, prompting conservative attacks. Glenn Beck said that "she's also making a run for the best actress nomination."[103] It's hard to imagine a similar line of attack against a male politician whose emotions flared in public, let alone wept – as GOP House Speaker John Boehner has done on multiple occasions.

Such sexism was a constant feature of the conservative critique of Clinton, even among conservative women. In October, after she took responsibility for the Benghazi attacks as head of the State Department, former National Organization for Women Los Angeles President turned right-wing radio host Tammy Bruce tweeted, "Liberal women are *trained* to be victims & she *owns* the results of her decisions." Conservative radio host Dana Loesch, then a CNN contributor, claimed at the same time that "Hillary Clinton is the Democrats' battered woman."[104]

The right had been promoting the importance of Clinton's testimony for weeks – and yet neither the questions from her Republican inquisitors nor her answers had revealed anything remotely like the grand conspiracy promised over the conservative airways. Even Fox News' Brit Hume called the hearings "meandering and unfocused" and said that Clinton "dominate[d]"[105] the proceedings.

Still, the sound bite — sometimes edited, always out of context – has managed to live on for months on right-wing talk radio shows: Clinton saying in elevated, anguished tones, "What difference at this point does it make?!" The frequent abuse of the short sound clip captures the petty essence of the Benghazi hoax. Meanwhile, back inside their idea lab, right-wing alchemists continued to re-engineer their distortion scheme for the next rollout.

Hoax VIII: A Disengaged Administration

Just one month later, conservatives were back on the Benghazi case – pursuing yet another line of attack. Like most of the others, it was based on speculation rather than any established facts. Investigators didn't have a minute-by-minute accounting of President Obama's activities on the night of September 11 or the morning of September 12 – or for Secretary of State Clinton, for that matter. Some conservatives embarked on a mission to prove that the top leaders had checked out, that neither Obama nor Clinton was up for the difficult work of fighting terrorism.

This was like other pieces of the Benghazi hoax. It was a conspiracy that hung largely on one fragment of evidence, and it came up again on the GOP scandal "Twister wheel" months after it should have been resolved. The resurrection started on February 7, when Defense Secretary Leon Panetta and Joint Chiefs of Staff Chairman Martin Dempsey testified before a Senate hearing on their interactions with the White House during the night of the Benghazi attacks. Both men were senior statesmen with national security gravitas, earned by Panetta as Bill Clinton's chief of staff and as Obama's CIA director, and Dempsey from a decades-long rise through the ranks that included major duties in the Iraq War. Each had played a key role in responding to the Benghazi attacks.

Under Sen. Kelly Ayotte's questioning, both acknowledged that following an initial meeting with the president, neither had spoken directly to him again that night. To conservatives, this was the "tell" that Obama had been disengaged. As the tidbit was told and re-told in the right-wing media, the president's alleged lack of interest in Benghazi grew in proportion – despite the lack of any new details.[106]

Fox News contributor Michael Goodwin claimed in a February *New York*

Post column, "According to Panetta, President Obama checked in with his military team early on during the attack, then checked out for the rest of the night. The next day, we already knew, he blamed the video maker and flew to Las Vegas for a campaign event."[107]

Michael Barone of the *Washington Examiner* engaged in the same line of attack in a February column: "Obama apparently wasn't curious about what was happening in Benghazi. He wasn't too concerned either the next morning, when after the first murder of a U.S. ambassador in 33 years, he jetted off on a four-hour ride to a campaign event in Las Vegas. I don't think you have to be a Republican partisan to consider that unseemly."[108]

Conservatives would later add other prominent figures to the list of administration members who had allegedly been disengaged that night. Monica Crowley summed up this argument on Fox during a May appearance, stating that "the two leaders of the U.S. government," the president and Hillary Clinton, were "unaccounted for that night. We have no narrative of where they were or what they were doing."[109]

As usual, the truth was hiding in plain sight. In fact, during that February 7 hearing, Panetta and Dempsey testified that they were with Obama when he was first told of the attack and that he instructed them to respond immediately and deploy all available forces as quickly as possible. Dempsey said that while he hadn't spoken directly to the president after that meeting, "I wouldn't say there was no follow-up from the White House. There was no follow-up, to my knowledge, with the president. But his staff was engaged with the national military command center pretty constantly through the period, which is the way it would normally work."[110] Panetta added that "The president is well-informed about what is going on; make no mistake about it."[111]

As for Clinton and Obama's then-national security adviser Tom Donilon, Hillary Clinton said during her own January 23 Senate testimony that she "spoke to the national security adviser, Tom Donilon, several times.

I briefed him on developments. I sought all possible support from the White House, which they quickly provided." In addition, Clinton testified that she spoke with then-CIA director Petraeus as well as the current head of the Libyan National Congress, and "I participated in a secure video conference of senior officials from the intelligence community, the White House, and DOD. We were going over every possible option, reviewing all that was available to us. Any actions we could take."

The secretary of state continued: "I spoke with President Obama later in the evening, to, you know, bring him up to date, to hear his perspective. Obviously, we kept talking with everyone during the night. Early in the morning, on the 12th, I spoke with General Dempsey, again, with Tom Donilon."[112]

Benghazi "whistleblower" Gregory Hicks, who served as the second in command (behind Ambassador Chris Stevens) of the U.S. delegation to Libya at the time of the attacks, would confirm Clinton's engagement that night, testifying during his May 8 appearance before the House Oversight Committee that at approximately 2 a.m., "Secretary of State Clinton called me along with her senior staff. . . . And she asked me what was going on, and I briefed her on developments."[113]

The extension of the "disengaged" questions to include Donilon provided a rare moment of humor in the right's relentless promotion of the Benghazi hoax. On May 30, *Fox & Friends* co-host Brian Kilmeade stated that "no one seemed to know where [Donilon] was" during the attacks in Benghazi, asking, "Where was he that night?" On-screen text during the segment asked, "Where Was Donilon On Night Of Benghazi?"

Above the text, Fox News was showing a picture of Donilon meeting with the president in the Oval Office on the night of Benghazi.[114]

That hilarious mix-up was, in a sense, a grand metaphor for a so-called administration "cover-up" of what in fact was arguably becoming the most thoroughly investigated event of its scope in decades. Over the course of just one year, administration officials held upwards of 40 briefings on Capitol Hill. They turned over footage from closed-circuit TVs and from unmanned aerial vehicles, or drones. Government staffers – both the highest ranking and those on the ground – have testified at more than 18 committee hearings so far, and conducted many more interviews with the House Committee on Oversight and Government Reform. They've produced reams of letters and documents – at least 25,000 pages, according to one source with knowledge of the information handed to investigators we spoke to.

If that's a cover-up, it's one of the more poorly executed – and one of the most transparent – cover-ups in American history.

Hoax IX: Military Options

In late April, Fox News' flagship news program, *Special Report*, featured a three-part interview with someone they described as a "military special ops member who watched as the deadly attack on the U.S. Consulate in Benghazi unfolded" to claim that the administration had the resources to provide additional military support in Benghazi but had neglected to do so. Interviewed with the dramatic flair of a dark shadow covering his face, the source claimed: "I know for a fact that [Special Forces team] C-110, the EUCOM CIF, was doing a training exercise in ... not in the region of North Africa, but in Europe ... And they had the ability to act and to respond."[115]

It was a compelling argument, especially for a typical news consumer who possesses only a casual knowledge of military affairs. Although Libya itself had been long isolated from the United States during the decades of dictatorship under Col. Moammar Gadhafi, the American military had bases in Europe, including nearby Italy, as well as throughout the Middle East and in Africa – not to mention the Navy's 6th Fleet in the Mediterranean Sea. Given the duration of the attack on the Benghazi compound, which began on the night of September 11 and lasted well into the next morning, surely there were additional forces that could have been deployed, possibly preventing the second wave of casualties at the annex to the compound.

Sen. John McCain – the former Vietnam Navy pilot and prisoner of war who had long presented himself as a knowledgeable source on military affairs – said during a Senate Armed Services Committee hearing in February, "We could have placed forces there. We could have had aircraft and other capabilities a short distance away at Souda Bay, Crete."[116]

Former Reagan speechwriter Peggy Noonan attacked the administration in *The Wall Street Journal*, writing in May, "So you don't launch a military rescue operation, you don't scramble jets, and you have a rationalization—they're too far away, they'll never make it in time. This was probably true, but why not take the chance when American lives are at stake?"[117]

After an Oversight and Government Reform hearing, Darrell Issa launched a similar line of attack, telling CNN that such forces "may not have arrived in time to save lives, but at the time the decision was made, the decision was wrong."[118] The assumption was not that military action would have actually made a difference, but still, why not attempt a rescue operation while the scenario was still uncertain?

Military experts, however, dismissed these notions. Robert Gates, secretary of defense during the Bush and Obama administrations, responded to the notion of further rescue operations by saying it was based on "sort of a cartoonish impression of military capabilities and military forces."[119] According to Gates: "We don't have a ready force standing by in the Middle East ... with planes on strip alert, troops ready to deploy at a moment's notice."

The former secretary of defense was similarly skeptical of the idea that the military should have used fighter jets to buzz the compound, a regular complaint of McCain and other conservative critics. "[G]iven the number of surface to air missiles that have disappeared from Gaddafi's arsenals," Gates said, "I would not have approved sending an aircraft, a single aircraft – over Benghazi under those circumstances."[120]

Explaining why more airpower wasn't deployed, former Secretary of Defense Leon Panetta said during February congressional testimony: "The reason simply is because armed UAVs, AC-130 gunships or fixed-wing fighters, with the associated tanking, you've got to provide air refueling abilities; you've got to arm all the weapons before you put them on the planes; targeting and support facilities, were not in the vicinity of Libya. And because of the distance, it would have taken at least nine to 12 hours, if not more, to deploy these forces to Benghazi."[121]

In other words, the suggested military operations would not have saved lives – they could have meant additional U.S. deaths, if a plane had been shot down, or even resulted in the nightmare of an American flyer taken prisoner by a terrorist group. Even the Republican chairmen of the five House committees investigating the Benghazi attack contradicted the notion that military assets were prevented from being deployed. In a clearly partisan report released in April, they wrote, "The evidence also does not show there were armed air assets above Benghazi at any time or that any such assets were called off from assisting U.S. personnel on the ground." The report added, "No evidence has been provided to suggest these officials refused to deploy resources because they thought the situation had been sufficiently resolved."[122]

Hoax X: The "Critical Cables"

On April 23, the Republican chairmen of five House committees, led by Issa, released a Benghazi report that was a direct assault on the legacy and the political reputation of former Secretary of State Hillary Clinton. The allegations raised against Clinton were so harsh that if they were to gain credence and spread widely through the mainstream media, they would have the potential to kill off a future electoral run before it starts.

The House report mentioned Clinton's name 30 times; Obama was referenced only 11 times. The very first bullet of the report's executive summary made clear who the Republicans were now focused upon: "Reductions of security levels prior to the attacks in Benghazi were approved at the highest levels of the State Department, up to and including Secretary Clinton. This fact contradicts her testimony before the House Foreign Affairs Committee on January 23, 2013." The House committees were accusing Clinton not only of being responsible for leaving the Benghazi diplomatic facility without sufficient defenses, but of perjuring herself before Congress.[123]

The Benghazi hoax was roughly eight months old, and it had been totally re-invented. The questions about Obama – about whether he was disengaged, didn't see the Benghazi attacks as terrorism, or orchestrated a cover-up with the help of Susan Rice – had eased up somewhat, at least on Capitol Hill, as the echoes of his second inaugural speech faded out. Although Republicans were undoubtedly still interested in disrupting the president's second-term agenda, the real passion for probing Benghazi had shifted toward Clinton – raising the question of whether the purpose was really improving diplomatic security or simply fomenting political chaos.

It signaled both a new direction for the right wing – and an old one. Although Clinton had long been a bête noire for conservatives right through her 2008 primary campaign against Obama, their criticism had let up during the president's first term. Hillary was also once again incredibly popular among Democrats, even those who had supported Obama in the primaries, and she had gained the respect and admiration of many in the center of the political spectrum. She was arguably the most popular political figure in the country. Even some Republicans were forced to offer grudging respect for her boundless energy as she trotted around the globe on diplomatic missions.

Things changed quickly when Clinton walked out of Foggy Bottom as secretary for the last time on February 1. Nothing was more important to Republicans, after all, than regaining the White House in 2016 after eight years of Democratic rule, and there was no greater roadblock than the popularity of the former first lady. Benghazi was the opportunity to hang an albatross around Hillary's neck and perhaps remind voters of the scandal-plagued 1990s, when conservative operatives intent on taking down her husband's presidency had woven claims out of whole cloth, claims shown to be false only after they had damaged the Clintons.

The new report's smoking gun on Clinton was two documents the report described as "critical cables" dealing with security in Benghazi. The first was a March 28, 2012, cable that then-U.S. Ambassador to Libya Gene Cretz sent "to Secretary Clinton" seeking additional security resources in Libya. The second was the April 19, 2012, response to Cretz, "bearing Secretary Clinton's signature," that "acknowledged then-Ambassador Cretz's formal request for additional security assets but ordered the withdrawal of security elements to proceed as planned" from the U.S. Mission in Libya, including in Benghazi.[124]

"Multiple committees have reviewed the State Department documents cited in the previous sections and remain concerned that the documents do not reconcile with public comments Secretary Clinton made regarding how high in the State Department the security situation and requests were discussed," the report states. According to the House committees, "[d]espite acknowledging a security request made on April 19, 2012," Clinton contradicted her January 23 testimony before the House Foreign Affairs Committee, during which she had said, "I have made it very clear that the security cables did not come to my attention or above the assistant secretary level where the ARB" – the review commissioned by the State Department – "placed responsibility."

From the outset, Hillary Clinton had successfully navigated criticism over her role in what had gone wrong in Benghazi. In an interview with CNN a month after the attacks, Clinton said, "I take responsibility. I'm in charge of the State Department's 60,000-plus people all over the world, 275 posts. The president and the vice president wouldn't be knowledgeable about specific decisions that are made by security professionals. They're the ones who weigh all of the threats and the risks and the needs and make a considered decision."[125]

But now, the accusation that Hillary Clinton knew much more about security risks at Benghazi than she had let on and had misled Congress during her closely watched testimony was too appealing a story for many journalists to pass up. Mainstream outlets like CNN[126], CBS News[127], and *Politico*[128] all quickly picked up the story, trumpeting the GOP allegations.

On *Fox & Friends* the day after the report's release, Issa gloated: "The secretary of state was just wrong. She said she did not participate in this, and yet only a few months before the attack, she outright denied security in her signature in a cable, April 2012."

Co-host Brian Kilmeade retorted that the cable, "sharply contradicts her sworn testimony. ... [I]t is in direct contradiction of what she told everybody, told the country."[129] Conservative media would trumpet the attack in the days to come. "Hillary Lied, And Four Died in Benghazi,"[130] read the headline for an *Investor's Business Daily's* editorial.

The GOP claim was described as "damning"[131] at TownHall.com, and a "bombshell"[132] on Fox Nation.

Sen. Rand Paul (R-KY) confirmed the aim of many Republican partisans in a May op-ed that cited Clinton's supposed role in cutting security in Benghazi as a reason that "Mrs. Clinton should never hold high office again."[133] That same month, Karl Rove's super PAC launched its first foray into the 2016 presidential race with a 90-second web ad titled "Benghazi" that rehashed many of the right's accusations about the attack. The fact that Barack Obama was not a major figure in the ad was noticed by John Avlon at The Daily Beast, who observed, "in Rove's video, the culprit is not Obama administration policy, but Clinton."[134] Speaking with Charlie Rose on May 29, 2013, *Politico* reporter Mike Allen revealed the true motivation behind the continued conservative obsession with the Benghazi attack. "Privately, Republicans say that Benghazi probably wouldn't be an issue if it weren't for Hillary Clinton,"[135] said the veteran journalist. A lethal tragedy had become a political shell game, its "prize" continually shuffled around. Now it was Hillary.

But one thing has remained constant for two decades: The desire to win at the so-called "politics of personal destruction," always precluding the facts. This time, the Republican attacks on Clinton's supposed role in decreasing security at diplomatic facilities in Libya were driven by a basic misunderstanding of State Department protocol. For one thing, if these cables were meant to be some kind of "smoking gun," they had been hiding in plain site. The House Oversight committee had posted the March 2012 cable on its own website before its October 2012 hearing.

Glenn Kessler of *The Washington Post*, who covered the State Department for nine years, reviewed Issa's comments on *Fox & Friends* for his Fact Checker blog. He pointed out that in the modern era, "cables" are really "group emails, which are stored in a database and made available to people with proper security clearances." As part of State Department protocol, Kessler explained, "every single cable from Washington gets the secretary's name at the bottom, even if the secretary happens to be on the other side of the world at the time."[136]

Kessler quoted a State Department spokesman's explanation that under this protocol, Clinton "'signed' hundreds of thousands of cables during her tenure as secretary. As then-Secretary Clinton testified, the security cables related to Benghazi did not come to her attention. These cables were reviewed at the assistant secretary level."

The Washington Post fact-checker also provided a lengthy list of cables dealing with extremely minor issues that had also been "signed" by Clinton and quoted several veterans from the Bush administration who explained that secretaries of state "sign" far more cables than they review. He concluded that Issa's statement "relies on an absurd understanding of the word 'signature' " and that the GOP chairman "has no basis or evidence to show that Clinton has anything to do with this cable" and thus had engaged in "inflammatory and reckless language."

Kessler called Issa's claim "absurd." He gave it Four Pinocchios – the blog's worst rating for truthfulness: a "whopper."

Hoax XI:
Attacks On The Accounability Review Board

A lot happened in the six months after the Benghazi attacks. Most notably, of course, the re-election of President Obama, but also the tragic mass shooting at an elementary school in Newtown, Connecticut – and while a half a year is not a long time, some of the earlier developments in the Benghazi saga were surely hazy to the news consumer. The ferocity of the GOP investigations in Washington, especially the new focus on Hillary Clinton, obscured the fact that a major investigation of what transpired before, during, and after September 11, 2012, had already taken place. In fact, the report from the State Department-com- missioned Accountability Review Board, or ARB, an independent investigation ordered in wake of the attacks, using a procedure set out by Congress under a 1986 antiterrorism law, actually did make recommendations for improving the safety of diplomats, and several State Department employees were disciplined for their mistakes. But that report and its critical information were of little or no use to Republicans and their new, ambitious political agenda. So instead, they attempted to trash it.

Ironically, when the ARB report was initially released in December 2012, leading Republicans largely hailed the document as a thorough and tough-minded look at what had happened. Writing in the conservative *Washington Times*, hawkish Senators John McCain, Lindsay Graham, and Kelly Ayotte said the paper "sheds important light on some of the failings within the State Department."[137] Those findings had been widely discussed by the co-chairs – Ambassador Thomas Pickering and Admiral Mike Mullen – in both a press conference and in briefings for staffers on the House Foreign Affairs Committee and the Senate Foreign Relations Committee. It was only after other avenues of political attack had been exhausted that GOP activists on Capitol Hill flip-flopped and portrayed the ARB report as a whitewash.

In their April report, the Republican chairmen of the five House committees that had reviewed Benghazi sought to undermine the conclusions of the ARB. The GOP report stated that the board "failed to conduct an appropriately thorough and independent review of which officials bear responsibility for those decisions."[138]

Primarily, the GOP chairmen criticized the ARB for failing to cast enough blame for the attack on Hillary Clinton. They also faulted the ARB for having "failed to provide a satisfactory explanation as to why it did not interview Secretary Clinton" in the course of its investigation.

Other conservatives quickly picked up the thread. "Instead of letting the facts lead the direction of the investigation, the report appears designed to protect the interests of Hillary Clinton, the State Department higher ups, and the president," wrote Victoria Toensing, the attorney for Benghazi "whistleblower" Greg Hicks, in a *Weekly Standard* blog post.[139] "[W]hy would we take [the ARB's co-chairman] seriously on anything if he doesn't even ask the pertinent questions to Hillary Clinton?" asked host Bill O'Reilly on his Fox program.[140]

Clinton had officially launched the Accountability Review Board investigation in the weeks after the attack. The ARB process is standard procedure after major attacks on State Department facilities; one took place after the deadly 1983 attacks on the U.S. Marine barracks in Beirut, Lebanon, and, more recently, an ARB was convened after a 2004 attack on an American consulate in Jeddah, Saudi Arabia, killed nine people. The inquiry was led by former Ambassador Thomas Pickering and retired Adm. Mike Mullen, two figures with resumes beyond reproach.

Pickering's service extended through five presidencies, during which he served as ambassador to Jordan, Nigeria, El Salvador, Israel, the United Nations, India, and Russia, as well as undersecretary of state for political affairs. Mullen served as chairman of the Joint Chiefs of Staff under both George W. Bush and Barack Obama, the capstone of a four-decade career in the Navy. Neither man had any reason to sully his reputation by carrying water for the Obama administration.

The board also consisted of Catherine Bertini, former executive director of the United Nations World Food Program; Richard Shinnick, a former State Department director for the Bureau of Overseas Buildings Operations; and Hugh Turner, representing the Intelligence Community from the CIA's Directorate of Operations. Like Pickering and Mullen, these participants had no motivation to risk their credibility on behalf of the administration.

As part of the ARB investigation, the board interviewed more than 100 parties in all different levels of government. Their report found that "[s]ystemic failures and leadership and management deficiencies at senior levels within two bureaus of the State Department resulted in a Special Mission security posture that was inadequate for Benghazi and grossly inadequate to deal with the attack that took place."[141]

The report was particularly critical of the security staffing decisions made by bureaus at the State Department.

It found that "certain senior State Department officials within two bureaus demonstrated a lack of proactive leadership and management ability in their responses to security concerns posed by Special Mission Benghazi, given the deteriorating threat environment and the lack of reliable host government protection"[142]

As a result, four staffers – Eric J. Boswell, assistant secretary for diplomatic security, Scott P. Bultrowicz, director of the Diplomatic Security Service, Charlene R. Lamb, deputy assistant secretary for diplomatic security, and Raymond Maxwell, deputy assistant secretary for North Africa – were placed on administrative leave. (After John Kerry became secretary of state, it was announced that all four would return to work at the State Department because the ARB did not find that any of them had "breached their duty or should be fired.")[143]

The report made 29 recommendations for policy changes at both the White House and State Department level and was a fair and accurate account of what took place in Libya. The Obama administration had done exactly what any citizen would expect of its government – investigated an overseas security breach in depth. The report's aim was mainly to offer corrective measures. Indeed, Clinton told lawmakers in January 2012 that 64 action items had been created from the findings, and the vast majority of them had been implemented or were being carried out at the time of her testimony. It was not a politically motivated document, nor did it leave blame on the doorsteps of the president or secretary of state. For this reason alone, it came under attack from conservatives who sought to discredit it, convinced that it had to be a whitewash.

Pickering addressed the decision not to formally interview Clinton during a May 12 appearance on *Meet the Press*: "We had a session with the secretary. It took place very near the end of the report. It took place when we had preliminary judgments about who made the decisions, where they were made, and by whom they were reviewed. We felt that that was more than sufficient for the preponderance of evidence that we had collected to make our decisions."[144]

But to Republicans who were hoping for a kind of Spanish Inquisition of the secretary of state, this was not a satisfactory answer. When new Secretary of State John Kerry reinstated the four State Department employees in August 2013, it sparked an angry outburst from Issa, who promised more investigations and claimed that State had decided "not to pursue any accountability from anyone."[145]

But considering the investigation's goal was to provide information to prevent an attack from occurring in the future, not to extract political rewards, the ARB's methods made sense. In now seeking to investigate an investigation, Republicans like Issa had moved far, far away from seeking diplomatic security solutions. The absurdity of this was driven home yet again on September 4, 2013, when *Fox & Friends* co-host Steve Doocy claimed that Undersecretary of State for Management Patrick Kennedy is somebody "we haven't heard from"[146] regarding Benghazi – when of course he had testified before the ARB.

Hoax XII: Muzzled

In mid-April came a report from Sharyl Attkisson of CBS News that "multiple new whistleblowers [were] privately speaking" to congressional investigators about the Benghazi attacks. This seemed to be a dream come true for President Obama and Hillary Clinton's conservative bashers who had long harbored fantasies that some people out there knew the real story of administration fecklessness in Libya, if the investigators could only get to them.[147]

And the fact that the story had broken on CBS News – the network of Walter Cronkite and the first in-depth TV report on the Watergate scandal – made the report all the more tantalizing to those on the right. It mattered not that the reporter, Attkisson, had been criticized in the past for questionable reporting, including broadcasting stories about the utterly discredited idea that there is some kind of a connection between vaccines and autism, long after such a link had been debunked.[148]

But the next week, House Oversight Chairman Darrell Issa released a statement stating that his panel would hold a hearing in May to "examine evidence that Obama administration officials have attempted to suppress information about errors and reckless misjudgments." The California Republican promised the hearing would "examine new facts about what happened and significant problems with the administration's own review of Benghazi failures."[149] After so many months of false starts, the right saw that its Benghazi hoax was finally – finally – gaining traction in the mainstream media.

Soon, conservatives began circulating claims that the administration had tried to suppress the testimonies of those whistleblowers. "I'm not talking generally, I'm talking specifically about Benghazi – that people have been threatened. And not just the State Department. People have been threatened at the CIA," said Victoria Toensing, the attorney for the most prominent "whistleblower," told Fox News in late April.[150]

Toensing's client was the career foreign service officer Gregory Hicks, who certainly came off as a sympathetic figure, and someone who was in the loop on Benghazi. Hicks had served as the deputy chief of mission for the U.S. delegation to Libya. From Tripoli, he had spoken to Ambassador Chris Stevens as the attack was underway and had reported in to Hillary Clinton later that night. Now, Hicks wanted to go on the record with criticisms of Clinton and the State Department in testimony before the House Oversight Committee, which detractors of the Obama administration were promised would blow the scandal open.

His attorney built up the expectations. "It's frightening, and they're doing some very despicable threats to people," Toensing told Fox. "Not 'we're going to kill you,' or not 'we're going to prosecute you tomorrow,' but they're taking career people and making them well aware that their careers will be over [if they cooperate with congressional investigators]."

The looming drama seemed so great that Fox News' Ed Henry even took the matter directly to President Obama during a White House press conference. "On the Benghazi portion [of the question], I know pieces of the story have been litigated and you've been asked about it." The conservative-tilting network's White House correspondent continued: "But there are people in your own State Department saying they've been blocked from coming forward, that they survived the terror attack and they want to tell their story. Will you help them come forward and just say it once and for all?"[151]

The president replied he was "not familiar" with what Henry was talking about. On Fox, contributors scoffed at that statement. "This is slightly incredible. It's a rather weak response for the president," said Charles Krauthammer. "Call me skeptical." "It clearly looks that the administration is engaged in at the very least obfuscation if not an actual cover-up," chimed in Stephen Hayes.[152] Conservative commentators were so caught up in their own echo chamber they couldn't accept that the president of the United States wasn't following all the ins and outs of their trumped-up scandal as discussed endlessly on their TV network – or that he wouldn't be "familiar" otherwise with the silencing of whistleblowers that wasn't actually taking place.

During an appearance on a right-wing talk radio show, Toensing raised the stakes by insisting that that Hicks had been "demoted" and that the administration was now claiming Hicks "had sought the desk job that he describes as a demotion" when in reality, "He was offered a choice: no job, or this job that doesn't mean anything."[153]

Hicks' testimony was set up to be a watershed moment in what the right was still portraying as the Benghazi scandal. He was portrayed as the deceased ambassador's loyal No. 2 who had been barred from speaking about the attacks and had been demoted and threatened when he tried to do so.

But during his public testimony, the high expectations quickly fizzled. Hicks made clear that he had actually already spoken with a variety of investigative bodies. Asked by Rep. John Mica (R-FL) whether he had been interviewed by the State Department Accountability Review Board that investigated the attacks, Hicks acknowledged that he had.

"Were you able to convey all information that you thought was necessary regarding this incident to the board?" Mica asked.

"The interview took about two hours, and it was in my mind incomplete. A few days later I had a separate meeting, briefly, with the executive secretary," Hicks replied, adding that the meeting was "to amplify on some issues that had been discussed at the meeting. At the initial interview."

The whistleblower also spoke with the FBI for its investigation of the attack.[154]

Hicks actually contradicted the assessment of his attorney that he had been given his current job as a punishment, telling the committee: "[M]y family really didn't want me to go back. We'd endured a year of separation when I was in Afghanistan 2006 and 2007. That was the overriding factor. So I voluntarily curtailed – I accepted an offer of what's called a no-fault curtailment." Hicks explained, "That means that there's – there would be no criticism of my departure of post, no negative repercussions."[155]

The Washington Post further reported that Hicks retained the same salary and rank in the department.[156] His new assignment was of a lower grade, but that is primarily because he left his post mid-appointment, at a time when few suitable slots are available for someone with his experience.

The most noteworthy allegation that caused a brief stir in the media came when he testified during the hearing that the State Department had ordered him "not to allow" himself and his colleagues "to be personally interviewed" by Republican Rep. Jason Chaffetz during the congressman's fact-finding mission to Libya. Some conservatives interpreted this to mean that he had been ordered not to communicate with the congressman at all. "Whistleblower: Hillary's State Dept. Told Me Not To Talk To Congress," Breitbart News' headline blared.[157]

But later in the hearing, Hicks made clear that this wasn't really the issue – he had actually been told not to talk to Chaffetz *without a State Department lawyer present*. *The New York Times* reported that a "State Department official said Mr. Hicks had been free to talk to Mr. Chaffetz, but that department policy required a department lawyer to be present during interviews for any Congressional investigation."

Hicks' much-ballyhooed testimony would provide little new information. "[T]he testimony did not fundamentally challenge the facts and timeline of the Benghazi attack and the administration's response to it," *The New York Times* reported.[158] While congressional Republicans had portrayed him as their "star witness," "Hicks was of little use to

Republicans in their efforts to connect the lapses in the Benghazi response to Clinton or the Obama White House," agreed Dana Milbank of the *The Washington Post.*[159] The GOP had cried wolf yet again.

Following the hearing, conservatives looked to save face by jumping on a portion of Hicks' testimony to claim that he had been the subject of an angry phone call from Cheryl Mills, Hillary Clinton's chief of staff at the State Department, complaining of his meeting with Chaffetz. Mills has worked for the Clintons on and off since the early 1990s and is known to be loyal to them. By tying Mills to an alleged attempt to intimidate a whistleblower, the right-wing media believed it had brought their scandal to Clinton's front door, if not to Clinton herself.

Sean Hannity said on May 10 that "Hicks was excoriated by Hillary's chief of staff Cheryl Mills for daring to talk to Chaffetz without an attorney." That same day, on Fox News' *Special Report*, Chris Wallace said Mills was "the person who apparently reprimanded Gregory Hicks for saying what he said." Fox News' Andrea Tantaros said on *The Five* that Mills "punished Hicks and demoted him allegedly and wanted to muscle him."

In fact, Hicks explained during the hearing that he only thought that Mills "was very upset" that the State Department attorney had not sat in on his interview with Chaffetz because "a phone call from that senior of a person is, generally speaking, not considered to be good news."[160]

But when questioned by Democratic Rep. Carolyn Maloney of New York, Hicks later clarified: "The statement was clearly no direct criticism, but the tone of the conversation – and again, this is part of the Department of State culture – the fact that she called me and the tone of her voice – and we're trained to gauge tone and nuance in language – indicated to me very strongly that she was unhappy."

One bizarre aspect of the allegation that key personnel had been "muzzled" is the fact that arguably the most important witnesses of all –

the five diplomatic security agents who survived the initial attack on the compound – testified to the FBI and the ARB. The reason these agents have sought anonymity is a desire to get on with their lives, including one agent who has returned to duty in the region. This desire to keep their names from the public eye was honored in the widely publicized book *Under Fire* by Fred Burton and Samuel Katz. More proof that no one was "muzzled" had come in October 2012 when Eric Nordstrom, the top regional security official in Libya, criticized State Department higher-ups for rebuffing his requests for additional forces.

A dozen attempts at fomenting scandal over Benghazi had all fizzled, some in spectacular, crash-and-burn fashion. It felt like the 1990s all over again, when conservatives – dubbed quite correctly, in hindsight, a "vast right-wing conspiracy" by Hillary Clinton – spent years and ultimately millions of taxpayer dollars in an effort to take down the presidency of Bill Clinton, combing through arcane land deals and making deplorable insinuations about the suicide of an administration official, Vincent Foster. One reason Benghazi felt the same was because so many of the players had not changed. The "whistleblower" Hicks' attorney, Toensing, along with her husband and law partner Joseph diGenova, had been deeply enmeshed in Republican efforts to destroy the Clinton presidency.

During the Bill Clinton era, Toensing and diGenova's efforts were so over the top that even fellow Republicans criticized them. Rep. Bill Clay of Missouri, ranking member of the Education and Workforce Committee whose Republican staff had hired the lawyers to investigate a campaign finance scandal involving the Teamsters, claimed, "the couple's relentless self-promotion and non-stop mugging for the likes of Geraldo Rivera - however good for business and their egos - is unseemly, undignified, unworthy of this committee and generally detrimental to important Congressional functions."[161] Now, nearly a generation later, the political popularity and endurance of another Clinton had caused some of the band to get back together – with Toensing and diGenova invited onto numerous shows to spread the Benghazi hoax. But their tune on this new coast-to-coast tour was every bit as jarring and off-key as before.

Hoax XIII: Left Behind

The Republican noise machine's buy-in to the Benghazi hoax has been dramatized by two related theories: that Obama and Clinton had somehow "left behind" the Americans who were under attack in Libya and, even worse, that a rescue mission was in the works and the administration had ordered it to "stand down." These new conspiracy theories had the feel of conservatives throwing them against the wall like spaghetti, looking to see what would stick. The ideas played to their fantasy notions of Obama, that the president was fundamentally weak on terrorism and didn't have the *cojones* to protect Americans when the chips were down.

"[F]or 237 years," Fox News host Eric Bolling claimed during a May 2013 appearance on Geraldo Rivera's radio show, the motto of the U.S. armed forces "is no one left behind. Leave no one behind. Leave no one under fire wanting or wondering if America was going to come back and help them. That's what Barack Obama, Hillary Clinton, and the administration did on September 11th of 2012. They left four Americans to die because they said 'stand down, don't go help,' and that is a problem."[162]

Actually, for most of America's history, this type of unsubstantiated political attack on the commander-in-chief would be considered beyond the pale. But within the bubble where President Obama's very legitimacy to serve has been under constant assault, the allegation was quickly echoed by others on the right. FrontPageMagazine.com spelled this out explicitly, claiming, "The Obama administration undoubtedly understood that its decision to leave defenseless Americans, including our ambassador, to needlessly die at the hands of al-Qaeda-linked jihadists would not go over well for a commander-in-chief in the throes of a presidential election and a secretary of state angling for the Oval Office in 2016."[163]

TownHall.com's Katie Pavlich, who made a name for herself in conservative circles investigating the scandal surrounding the U.S. Bureau of Alcohol, Tobacco, Firearms, and Explosives' botched arms sting called Operation Fast and Furious, wrote, "The men in Libya were left to die as military forces were told to stand down."[164]

On Fox News, national security analyst KT McFarland, who attempted to run against Hillary Clinton for her Senate seat in 2006, made a bizarre claim that there was a political decision to abandon those under attack in Benghazi. "I've got a guess that it's something that was a political decision," she said. "And not only a political decision not to give them the kind of security they wanted, but it was probably a political decision not to rescue them."[165] The question of what was to be gained politically by not trying to thwart an assault that killed four Americans – had such a counter-attack been logistically possible – hangs in the air.

Still, this baffling new argument took root with those most deeply engaged with preventing a successful Hillary Clinton campaign in 2016. Roger Ailes' personal attorney, Peter Johnson Jr., also suggested on Fox News that people within the Obama administration may have "sacrificed Americans based on a political calculation," and he was soon echoed by then-Fox News contributor Liz Cheney, who was preparing to run for the Senate in Wyoming.[166]

Lost in all the conservative chatter were the basic, well-known facts of what happened on the night of September 11 and the next morning. Recall that in stark contrast to the claims that no help had been sent by the Obama administration to aid Americans in Benghazi, a seven-man security team was scrambled from the Libyan capital of Tripoli immediately after it became clear the diplomatic facility had come under attack. In fact, one of the four American casualties in Benghazi, Glen Doherty, a former Navy SEAL, was a member of that rescue team.

The timeline is simple. Ambassador Christopher Stevens and Sean Smith, the information management officer at the Benghazi compound, were killed soon after the initial attack began at 9:30 p.m. local time, long before any rescue mission from anywhere outside Benghazi could have been mustered to save them. After 11 p.m., a lull in the fighting allowed a security team from the CIA annex that included former Navy SEAL and CIA security contractor Tyrone Woods to evacuate the diplomatic facility and return the survivors to the annex, where they holed up under intermittent fire and waited for more help to arrive.

The seven-man security team in Tripoli launched its rescue operation within minutes of the initial reports of an attack and chartered an aircraft as soon as possible in the dead of the Libyan night. This team, which included Doherty, now a CIA contractor, arrived at the Benghazi CIA annex at roughly 5 a.m. local time. Less than fifteen minutes later, the second engagement began. Woods and Doherty were killed during that roughly 10-minute attack when three mortar rounds hit the roof of the building within a span of 90 seconds.[167]

Twelve hours after the first attack began, all surviving American personnel had safely evacuated from Benghazi. With them they carried the bodies of those who perished. Not a single American was left behind. It was a night of loss but also feats of heroism that were rarely discussed by Republican leaders or conservative pundits because it undercut their storyline.

Daniel Benjamin, who ran the State counterterrorism bureau that headed the Foreign Emergency Support Team (FEST) at the time of the attack, said at the time of the May 2013 hearing that FEST had been aware of the situation in Benghazi but that using this unit was not a viable option.

"I can say now with certainty, as the former coordinator for counter-terrorism, that this charge is simply untrue," he said in a statement released by the State Department. "At no time did I feel that the bureau was in any way being left out of deliberations that it should have been part of."[168]

Hoax XIV: The Stand Down Order

Along with the bogus "left behind" claims came a slight variation of the same general idea: that armed forces who were ready to go into Benghazi that night were mysteriously ordered to "stand down" – presumably by someone at the highest levels and quite possibly by President Obama himself.

This was, for all intents and purposes, a conspiracy theory that was not only abetted but actively promoted by leaders of the Republican Party. Rep. Jason Chaffetz articulated this notion in an interview with Sean Hannity, telling the Fox host, "We had people that were getting killed, we had people who are willing to risk their lives to go save them and somebody told them to stand down."[169]

The backstory for this accusation will sound familiar. Chaffetz and other Republicans were basing their harsh accusation on a tiny sliver of testimony, spun into something else, then amplified and repeated dozens of times. Once again, it originated with the muddled April testimony from diplomat Gregory Hicks.

In a private interview with House Oversight Committee staffers prior to his public testimony, Hicks said that a second small team of CIA and DOD personnel and contractors had been preparing to board a plane leaving Tripoli for Benghazi when its commander, Lt. Col. S.E. Gibson, "got a phone call from SOCAFRICA which said, 'you can't go now, you don't have the authority to go now.' And so they missed the flight ... They were told not to board the flight, so they missed it."

When excerpts from the interview were released – likely by Republicans on the committee or their staffs – shortly before Hicks was scheduled to testify publicly, it would be spun as a "stand down" order that likely originated at the highest reaches of the Obama administration.[170] Note that even Hicks did not use the term "stand down" – but when the Issa-Chaffetz-led effort held its public hearings, this idea was embedded in their questioning as if it were a well-established fact.

During a televised hearing before the House Oversight Committee, Jason Chaffetz asked Hicks how personnel in Tripoli "react[ed] to being told to stand down."

Hicks replied, "They were furious." He went on to quote Lt. Col. S.E. Gibson, saying, "This is the first time in my career that a diplomat has more balls than somebody in the military."[171]

That sure sounded dramatic, and following Hicks' testimony, Oversight Committee Chairman Issa asked in a press release, "Who gave the order for special operations forces to stand down, preventing them from helping their compatriots under attack?"[172]

To Obama's detractors, this "stand-down order" proved their deeply rooted suspicion that the administration had refused to send help to U.S. personnel in harm's way, leading to their deaths. And they knew where they wanted to place the blame. "To a lot of people's understanding," explained *Fox & Friends* co-host Steve Doocy, "the only people who could say stand down would be the president of the United States or the secretary of defense."[173] In the weeks that followed, the audience for Fox's prime-time programming would hear the accusation that such an order had been given at least 85 times.[174]

In fact, no stand-down order had been given. Less than 90 minutes after the attacks began, then-Defense Secretary Leon Panetta and Chairman of the Joint Chiefs of Staff Gen. Martin Dempsey first briefed the president on the situation in Benghazi. According to Panetta, it was at this meeting that Obama ordered "all available DOD assets to respond to the attack in Libya and to protect U.S. personnel and interests in the region."[175]

Dempsey explained why Gibson's team hadn't been sent to Benghazi during a June 12 Senate Budget Committee hearing. He told New Hampshire Sen. Kelly Ayotte that the team that was supposedly told to "stand down" had actually been "told that the individuals in Benghazi were on their way back and that they would be better used at the Tripoli Airport – because one of them was a medic – that they would be better used to receive the casualties coming back from Benghazi and that if they had gone, they would have simply passed each other in the air, and that's the answer I received." Dempsey concluded, "They weren't told to stand down. A 'stand down' means don't do anything. They were told to – that the mission they were asked to perform was not in Benghazi but was at Tripoli Airport."[176]

In a June 26 closed hearing with the House Armed Services Committee, Lt. Col. Gibson himself denied having received a stand-down order. After the classified briefing with military officials including Gibson had concluded, the Republican-led committee released a statement saying, "Contrary to news reports, Gibson was not ordered to 'stand down' by higher command authorities in response to his understandable desire to lead a group of three other special forces soldiers to Benghazi."[177] In July, Gibson's testimony would be corroborated by his commanding officer, Col. George Bristol.[178]

Even if Gibson and his team of three soldiers had attempted to join the fighting, they would have saved no additional lives. According to Hicks' testimony, the plane that would have carried the team did not leave Tripoli until "sometime between 6:00 and 6:30 a.m." That departure time was at a minimum 45 minutes after the second attack on the CIA annex occurred.[179]

Unlike the bogus allegation that was broadcast 85 times on Fox News, the true, corrected version was not similarly trumpeted.

Hoax XV: Jonathan Karl's Scoop

The increasing background noise of the Benghazi hoax had not come close to landing a direct blow on anyone of importance within the Obama administration, but it was broadcast at so many decibels that eventually the mainstream media picked up the signal. This was clearly one of the goals of those on the far right promoting the Benghazi story, and its eventual success was not surprising or unprecedented. Conservative conspiracy-mongering had bled over into the conventional media – even the most prestigious news outlets like *The New York Times* – again and again during Bill Clinton's presidency, diverting public attention and journalistic resources into inconsequential stories like the Whitewater land deal. Reporters for established news outlets work with a healthy skepticism for the administration in power, but when Democrats are in the White House, conservatives have become adept at badgering a so-called "liberal media" to prove its lack of bias by adopting their story ideas.

The right-wing fixation over who edited the Benghazi talking points and how had continued long after Obama's re-election and the successful effort to cripple Susan Rice's possible secretary of state nomination. In May, the quest to discover who edited the Benghazi talking points led to an embarrassing controversy that ensnared ABC News reporter Jonathan Karl.

Karl was a respected reporter with a reputation for even-handedness. A 15-year veteran of Washington's congressional, State Department, and White House beats, Karl had been named ABC's chief White House correspondent in December 2012 and was regularly featured across the network's programming. A negative report on the administration from Karl would carry much more weight among other journalists than one from a conservative outlet that had been pushing the "scandal" line. In late spring, Karl turned his attention to the question of how the

Benghazi talking points used by Rice had been formulated.

"When it became clear last fall that the CIA's now discredited Benghazi talking points were flawed, the White House said repeatedly the documents were put together almost entirely by the intelligence community," Karl reported on May 10, "but White House documents reviewed by Congress suggest a different story."

"ABC News has obtained 12 different versions of the talking points that show they were extensively edited as they evolved from the drafts first written entirely by the CIA to the final version distributed to Congress and to U.S. Ambassador to the U.N. Susan Rice before she appeared on five talk shows the Sunday after that attack," Karl explained in his ABCNews.com exclusive. "White House emails reviewed by ABC News suggest the edits were made with extensive input from the State Department. The edits included requests from the State Department that references to the Al Qaeda-affiliated group Ansar al-Sharia be deleted as well [as] references to CIA warnings about terrorist threats in Benghazi in the months preceding the attack."[180]

Karl's report did contain new information. At the center were the emails written by State Department spokeswoman Victoria Nuland and Ben Rhodes, a White House deputy national security adviser, during the interagency process that produced the talking points. Nuland, a career foreign service officer, had been working at the State Department since the Reagan administration. She had served as principal deputy national security adviser to Vice President Dick Cheney and as the U.S. ambassador to NATO. She had a reputation as a consummate professional and an institutional loyalist, not a political or ideological partisan.

Rhodes, meanwhile, had worked for former Rep. Lee Hamilton (D-IN), helping to draft the Iraq Study Group report and the recommendations of the 9/11 Commission before taking a job as a speechwriter for then-Sen. Obama and working his way up through the campaign and White House communications shops.

In his report, Karl wrote that Nuland had criticized the original draft because it provided details about previous CIA warnings that "could be abused by members [of Congress] to beat up the State Department for not paying attention to warnings, so why would we want to feed that either?" According to Karl, Rhodes had responded to criticisms of the original talking points draft as follows:

> We must make sure that the talking points reflect all agency equities, including those of the State Department, and we don't want to undermine the FBI investigation. We thus will work through the talking points tomorrow morning at the Deputies Committee meeting.

According to Karl's report, "After that meeting, which took place Saturday morning at the White House, the CIA drafted the final version of the talking points – deleting all references to al Qaeda and to the security warnings in Benghazi prior to the attack." This was presented as a contradiction to White House Press Secretary Jay Carney's November statement that the intelligence community had been responsible for the talking points and that the White House had made only minor changes.[181] The implication was that Rhodes, contrary to the White House's assertion, stepped into a discussion between the State Department and the CIA, ordering the drafts to be rewritten to satisfy the State Department's concerns.

After Karl's report that the talking points had been "scrubbed of terror reference[s]," conservatives rushed to declare that these changes had been made for political reasons. With Rice out of the picture and Obama's re-election having already come to pass, they fixated yet again on their newfound strategy of using Benghazi to bring down Hillary Clinton. Whatever the real significance of the talking points back-and-forth revealed by Karl, conservatives grabbed their magnifying glasses and looked for Hillary.

On his Fox News program the night of Karl's report, Sean Hannity would highlight Nuland's email, play a clip of Clinton saying that "the intelligence community was the principal decider about what went into the talking points," then declare, "We now know that was a bold-faced lie because as we just showed you after one of Hillary's top advisors sent an email criticizing the official talking points, any and all references to Al Qaeda, terrorism, and any mention of CIA warnings that were issued prior to the attack, it was all scrubbed out of the talking points."[182] The same day, the Karl Rove-linked super PAC American Crossroads released a web ad attacking Clinton over her role in Benghazi. "I'd call it a cover-up," said John McCain on ABC's *This Week* two days later. "I would call it a cover-up in the extent that there was willful removal of information which was obvious," namely that the attack had been perpetrated by terrorists. He added that he thought Clinton "has played a role in this" and "had to have been in the loop some way"[183] on the editing of the talking points. Obama's losing 2008 GOP challenger even called for the creation of a select congressional committee to get to the bottom of it — an echo of the Watergate scandal that brought down Richard Nixon.[184] In reality, nothing in the heavily promoted ABC report disproved former CIA director David Petraeus' statement, discussed earlier, that the intelligence community signed off on the final draft of the talking points and that the reason that references to terrorist groups in Libya were removed was to avoid tipping off those groups.

Moreover, Karl's report suggested that the White House was trying to downplay the role that terrorism played for political reasons. That theory was at odds with President Obama's repeated reference to the attacks as an "act of terror" on September 12 and 13. Clinton herself had said on September 21, "What happened in Benghazi was a terrorist attack, and we will not rest until we have tracked down and brought to justice the terrorists who murdered four Americans."[185]

Thus Karl's only "exclusive" was the allegation that the emails he said weighed in on early drafts of the talking points amounted to a contradiction with Carney's November statement that the "talking points originated from the intelligence community," and that the White House had made only a single minor edit. But as Carney noted in a response included at the end of Karl's article, those emails had indicated "inputs" by the White House and State Department; the CIA had been the ones that "drafted these talking points and redrafted these talking points." Carney said that the only changes made by the White House were "stylistic and nonsubstantive." In the end, Karl's report turned on the distinction between "input" and "editing."

That doesn't exactly add up to Watergate. What's more, the key element of Karl's scoop was about to collapse.

Further scrutiny and reporting would reveal that Karl's source – assumed by observers to be a Republican staffer or member of one of the House committees investigating Benghazi – had given him misleading information to bolster the right-wing argument that the White House and State Department had teamed up to scrub the emails. Karl's reporting had downplayed and at times misled on the fact that he never actually saw any of the White House or State Department emails, but instead had a source read him summaries of those emails over the phone – a recipe for journalistic disaster.

Four days after Karl's initial report, CNN obtained an actual copy of the Rhodes email at the heart of the Karl report. According to CNN's Jake Tapper, that email "differs from how sources characterized it" to ABC and indicated that "whoever leaked it did so in a way that made it appear that the White House was primarily concerned with the State Department's desire to remove references and warnings about specific terrorist groups so as to not bring criticism to the department."[186] The actual text of the Rhodes email Karl had highlighted read:

> "Sorry to be late to this discussion. We need to resolve this in a way that respects all of the relevant equities, particularly the investigation.
>
> "There is a ton of wrong information getting out into the public

domain from Congress and people who are not particularly informed. Insofar as we have firmed up assessments that don't compromise intel or the investigation, we need to have the capability to correct the record, as there are significant policy and messaging ramifications that would flow from a hardened mis-impression.

"We can take this up tomorrow morning at deputies."

As Jake Tapper noted, "Whoever provided those accounts seemingly invented the notion that Rhodes wanted the concerns of the State Department specifically addressed."[187] The summaries Jonathan Karl published thus misinterpreted the actual text of the email, advancing the right wing's narrative. The full text of the email made clear that Rhodes wanted to ensure that the talking points were accurate and didn't compromise intelligence gathering methods or the investigation.

Karl subsequently released a statement saying, "I regret that one email was quoted incorrectly and I regret that it's become a distraction from the story, which still entirely stands." As Talking Points Memo's Josh Marshall would point out, this claim made no sense. "A central point of his story was White House involvement and White House involvement *on behalf of the State Department*," Marshall wrote. "The alleged quotes were key evidence for that claim but the quotes were wrong. Ergo, the story cannot 'entirely stand.' Calling this error a 'distraction' from the story is incorrect because the error undermines the story itself."[188]

Media observers would pillory Karl for the mistake in the days to come. The way Karl concealed the secondhand nature of his report was "highly problematic ethically, and the failure to acknowledge and correct is even worse," Edward Wasserman, dean of the Graduate School of Journalism at the University of California, Berkeley, told *Media Matters*.[189]

In response to Jonathan Karl's story, the White House ultimately released the entire chain of emails. Those emails filled in the gaps left by Karl's report, which had suggested that Nuland had called for changes to the talking points solely to prevent criticism of the State Department.

At several moments during the email chain, Nuland stepped into the conversation, first expressing concern that if the document were to cite "extremists," she and others would be asked by the media, "how do we know, who were they[?]"

The Nuland email cited by Karl actually raised concerns about giving recipients of the talking points information that could damage the investigation of the attack:

> On that basis, I have serious concerns about all the parts high-lighted below, and arming members of Congress to start making assertions to the media that we ourselves are not making because we don't want to prejudice the investigation.
>
> In same vein, why do we want Hill to be fingering Ansar al Sharia, when we aren't doing that ourselves until we have investigation results... and the penultimate point could be abused by Members to beat the State Department for not paying attention to Agency warnings so why do we want to feed that either? Concerned...

After minor edits were made by the FBI in response to her email, Nuland wrote back to the list: "These don't resolve all my issues or those of my building leadership."

This was when Ben Rhodes stepped in and suggested dealing with the talking points at a meeting the next day and said, "We need to resolve this in a way that respects all of the relevant equities, particularly the investigation."

After that Saturday morning meeting, the final major edits to the talking points were made by David Petraeus' deputy at the CIA, Mike Morell, who, according to administration officials, "acted on his own and not in response to pressure from the State Department" – just as Carney had said in the briefing room back in November.[190]

The Karl story had triggered a week of mainstream coverage of Benghazi, with even the major broadcast networks giving significant attention to the question of the talking points. But with the release of the full set of emails, *CBS Evening News* anchor Scott Pelley explained that while Republicans had claimed that they found "proof" that "the administration watered down the facts in talking points" for political reasons in the Karl story, "it turns out some of the quotes in those emails were wrong." Detailing the flaws in the GOP storyline, CBS White House correspondent Major Garrett explained, "There is no evidence, Scott, the White House orchestrated these changes."[191]

The mainstream media had gotten sucked too close to the flaming mass that was the Benghazi hoax, and it got burned.

Conclusion: "Benghazi, Benghazi, Benghazi"

"Let's start with Benghazi," shouted the man with the bullhorn.

It was a warm Thursday afternoon in late August in New Haven, Connecticut, and there were about a dozen people gathered on a large overpass at I-95, the main thoroughfare of the Eastern Seaboard. They were yelling and waving at passing cars behind two banners draped from the railing: The now familiar "Don't Tread on Me" Gadsden flag embraced by the Tea Party and a homemade sheet emblazoned with "Impeach Obama."

One of the pro-impeachment demonstrators named Denise Cassano was asked by the *New Haven Register* why she was protesting, and she began, "When there are 30 people who were trapped in a slaughter in Benghazi and no one has been interviewed…"[192] – the first of a litany of factually challenged complaints that are all well known to regular viewers of the Fox News Channel. The reality that virtually every official involved in Benghazi has been interviewed by the House or the Senate or the Accountability Review Board either did not register with Cassano, or it did not matter.

Oklahoman James Neighbors, who went on Facebook to organize Over-passes for Obama's Impeachment events across America, told *New York* magazine that if there was any issue that animated the people showing up, it was "Benghazi, Benghazi, Benghazi. I hope people go home and they look up Benghazi [after seeing it on a sign]," he said. "I hope they feel rage, and I hope they want to do something about it. I hope they demand their congressmen do something about it."[193]

Even more remarkably, a few right-wing members of Congress have been listening. Back in May, Sen. James Inhofe, also of Oklahoma,

.

told a nationally syndicated conservative radio show that as more information about Benghazi emerged, "People may be starting to use the I word before too long."[194]

"The I word meaning impeachment?" asked the show's host, Rusty Humphries.

"Yeah."

Really? More than a dozen half-baked or completely bogus allegations about the attack in Libya have been raised over the course of nearly a year, and each one has been debunked by credible sources. But that still was not enough for either the rank-and-file Tea Partiers or the extremists their districts have elected to Washington in recent years. After hearing literally hundreds of reports on Fox News or insinuations from talk-radio personalities about alleged wrongdoing in the name of Benghazi, it was hard for these partisans not to wonder why a president behind what they'd been informed was the worst scandal since the disgraced Richard Nixon was still in office.

But there was one thing about one year of the Benghazi hoax that was even more dismaying: The continued willingness of well-established and well-regarded news organizations to chase after the inflated scandalmongering of the extreme right – to go on the air asking leading questions that have already been asked and answered by independent or authoritative sources months earlier.

"[T]he military says, right, they couldn't have gotten to Benghazi in time, but the United States has the greatest military in the world," host Erin Burnett told CNN's audience on the night of August 6, 2013. "So, that seems shocking." Burnett was hosting a heavily promoted, hour-long special that promised viewers "The Truth About Benghazi."[195] What those who tuned in actually saw were 60 minutes with little new information – while several already disproved conspiracy theories were re-litigated for the umpteenth time. You'll recall, for example, that Burnett's question about a military response had been explained weeks earlier by the likes of former Bush-and-Obama Defense Secretary Robert Gates, who said it was based on a "cartoonish impression" of U.S. capabilities.

Yet that was not the only canard of the Benghazi hoax that was strangely reanimated by CNN in its August special. The chief reporter in the special, John King, once again raised the revisions to the talking points given to Susan Rice and asked whether "it was done just politically to protect the department? Or more nefariously" to shield the State Department or President Obama. There was no mention during the show of the testimony by ex-CIA chief Petraeus or the career diplomat Victoria Nuland that the omission of the names of specific terrorist groups was done so as to not tip them off as they were being investigated in connection to the attack. The CNN special also asked why America hadn't heeded specific warnings about the pending attack – when even conservative GOP Rep. Mike Rogers, the chairman of the House Intelligence Committee, joined others in confirming there simply had been no such warnings.

The CNN special did illustrate one thing: The willingness of a mainstream news organization to bend over backward to show its ideological "balance" and to treat the steady flow of Benghazi allegations seriously – even long after every hint of scandal about the events in Libya had proven to be a false lead. It once again showed the necessity of laying out each dead tentacle of the Benghazi hoax – and the actual facts that killed each one. Every minute wasted on these bogus allegations, not just by rabid partisans on the right, but by news directors and other "deciders" in the media, is a lost minute that could have been spent discussing more jobs, better schools, or saving the environment. In a free society like America, the only antidote to their untruthful noise is to speak the truth, just as loudly and with even greater force.

The reality is that there are two Benghazis. There is the Benghazi of right-wing legend – a state of mind, where they fantasize that a cartoon version of President Obama left American citizens to die, either from sheer cowardice or by fulfilling their bitter instinct that a commander-in-chief named Barack Hussein Obama would on some level sympathize with the wrong side in their never-ending war on terrorism. No wonder some of those who rally on overpasses for Obama's impeachment cannot likely locate this Benghazi on a map, because it is a mythical place – exploited by the high-def hucksters of cable-TV ratings and the GOP's scandal-industrial complex that doesn't think twice about twisting personal tragedy into political gain.

The amped-up volume of this Republican contraption has all but drowned out the real Benghazi, a city where noble Americans like Chris Stevens and Sean Smith volunteered to try to finish a U.S. mission that started a year before, when the Obama administration worked with our allies to rid Libya of Gadhafi's tyrannical regime and help bring democracy to a North African desert. They knew this assignment – imbued with American values, aimed at making life better for people halfway across the globe – carried enormous risk, and Stevens, Smith, Glen Doherty, and Tyrone Woods lost their lives trying to make it a reality. While partisan noisemakers schemed to create headlines, officials within the government have worked quietly but tirelessly at doing the responsible things – first rescuing the bulk of the Americans there, then burying and honoring the dead, then learning what went wrong to better protect U.S. diplomats, cooperating with congressional panels and implementing recommendations for better security, and finally, pursuing justice against the terrorists who carried out the attacks.[196]

That is in keeping with the promise that President Obama made to the grieving family members and friends of the murdered Americans at their memorial service: that the United States "will never retreat from the world."[197] It is this notion – of completing a worthy mission – that animates those who have no interest in the manipulations of a political hoax but who understand the real Benghazi. They share the sentiments of Ambassador Stevens' sister, the first family member that Secretary of State Clinton reached when she phoned to offer condolences.[198] Anne Stevens absorbed the details, paused, and said, "Don't let this stop the work he was doing."

Notes

1. "Obama Gains a Post-Convention Boost – But Not Among Likely Voters," ABC News/*Washington Post* poll, September 11, 2012, http://www.langerresearch.com/uploads/1140a1AftertheConventions.pdf.

2. Nate Silver, "Sept. 10: Will Obama's Convention Bounce Hold," *New York Times*, September 11, 2012, http://fivethirtyeight.blogs.nytimes.com/2012/09/11/sept-10-will-obamas-bounce-hold/.

3. William Kristol, "A Real War & a Phony War," *The Weekly Standard*, September 10, 2012; Volume 17, No. 48. http://www.weeklystandard.com/articles/real-war-phony-war_651386.html.

4. Gabriel Schoenfeld, *A Bad Day On the Romney Campaign: An Insider's Account* (New York: InterMix Books, 2013)

5. Ashley Parker, "After Criticism Of His Convention Speech, Romney Thanks Nation's Armed Forces," *New York Times*, September 11, 2012, http://www.nytimes.com/2012/09/12/us/politics/after-criticism-romney-thanks-armed-forces.html.

6. Fred Burton and Samuel M. Katz, *Vanity Fair*, August 2013, "40 Minutes in Benghazi." http://www.vanityfair.com/politics/2013/08/Benghazi-book-fred-burton-samuel-m-katz.

7. Significant Attacks Against U.S. Diplomatic Facilities and Personnel, United States Department of States, Bureau of Diplomatic Security. http://www.state.gov/documents/organization/211361.pdf.

8. Gabriel Schoenfeld, *A Bad Day On the Romney Campaign: An Insider's Account* (New York: InterMix Books, 2013).

9. Rick Gladstone, "Anti-American Protests Flare Beyond the Mideast," *New York Times*, September 14, 2012, http://www.nytimes.com/2012/09/15/world/middleeast/anti-american-protests-over-film-enter-4th-day.html?pagewanted=all.

10. Brooks Barnes, "Man Behind Anti-Islam Video Gets Prison Term," *New York Times*, November 7, 2012, http://www.nytimes.com/2012/11/08/us/maker-of-anti-islam-video-gets-prison-term.html.

11. Michael Joseph Gross, "Disaster Movie," VanityFair.com, December 27, 2012, http://www.vanityfair.com/culture/2012/12/making-of-innocence-of-muslims.

12. "What They Said, Before and After the Attack in Libya," NYTimes.com, September 12, 2012, http://www.nytimes.com/interactive/2012/09/12/us/politics/libya-statements.html?_r=0.

13. *Ibid.*

14. Text: Obama's Speech in Cairo, NYTimes.com, June 4, 2009, http://www.nytimes.com/2009/06/04/us/politics/04obama.text.html?pagewanted=3&_&_r=0.

15. "President Obama's Cairo Speech: Outrageous, Absurd, Embarrassing," RushLimbaugh.com, June 4, 2009, http://www.rushlimbaugh.com/daily/2009/06/04/president_obama_s_cairo_speech_outrageous_absurd_embarrassing.

16. Glenn Kessler, "Obama's 'Apology Tour,' " The Fact Checker, WashingtonPost.com, February 22, 2011, http://voices.washingtonpost.com/fact-checker/2011/02/obamas_apology_tour.html.

17. Luke Johnson, "John Sununu: 'I Wish This President Would Learn How To Be An American,' " HuffingtonPost.com, July 17, 2012, http://www.huffingtonpost.com/2012/07/17/john-sununu-obama_n_1679803.html.

18. Greg Sargent, "Top Romney adviser: 'Apology' statement fit our narrative, so we ran with it." The Plum Line, WashingtonPost.com, September 13, 2012, http://www.washingtonpost.com/blogs/plum-line/post/top-romney-adviser-apology-statement-fit-our-narrative-so-we-ran-with-it/2012/09/13/9e11293c-fdb9-11e1-b153-218509a954e1_blog.html.

19. *Ibid.*

20. Jack Mirkinson, "Mitt Romney Response to Libya, Egypt Attacks called 'Irresponsible,' 'Craven,' 'Ham-Handed.'" HuffingtonPost.com, September 12, 2012, http://www.huffingtonpost.com/2012/09/12/mitt-romney-libya-egypt-media-reactions_n_1877266.html.

21. Byron Tau, "Obama administration disavows Cairo 'apology.' " Politico.com, September 11, 2012, http://www.politico.com/politico44/2012/09/white-house-disavows-cairo-apology-135247.html.

22. "What They Said, Before and After the Attack in Libya," NYTimes.com, September 12, 2012, http://www.nytimes.com/interactive/2012/09/12/us/politics/libya-statements.html?_r=0.

23. *On the Record with Greta Van Susteren*, Fox News Channel, September 12, 2012, http://mediamatters.org/research/2012/09/13/right-wing-media-point-fingers-at-obama-for-lib/189885.

24. *Special Report*, Fox News Channel, September 12, 2012, http://www.foxnews.com/on-air/special-report-bret-baier/2012/09/13/all-star-panel-politics-embassy-attacks.

25. Hannity, Fox News Channel, September 12, 2012, http://mediamatters.org/research/2012/09/13/fox-rallies-around-romney-for-widely-criticized/189886.

26. "Remarks by the President on the Deaths of U.S. Embassy Staff in Libya," WhiteHouse.gov, September 12, 2012, http://www.whitehouse.gov/the-press-office/2012/09/12/remarks-president-deaths-us-embassy-staff-libya.

27. *Fox & Friends First*, Fox News Channel, September 13, 2012, http://mediamatters.org/research/2012/09/13/fox-rallies-around-romney-for-widely-criticized/189886.

28. "Romney's Foreign Policy Fumble Getting Notice In Battleground States," Democrats.org, September 14, 2012, http://www.democrats.org/news/press/romneys_foreign_policy_fumble_getting_notice_in_battle_ground_states.

29. *Ibid.*

30. *Ibid.*

31. Laura Meckler and Carol E. Lee, "Romney Gets Heat From Some Republicans," WSJ.com, September 12, 2012, http://blogs.wsj.com/washwire/2012/09/12/romney-gets-heat-from-some-republicans/.

32. *Ibid.*

33. Reid Pillifant, "On Romney's Libya comments, Pete King says he would have waited," CapitalNewYork.com, September 12, 2012, http://www.capitalnewyork.com/article/politics/2012/09/6537027/romneys-libya-comments-pete-king-says-he-would-have-waited.

34. Wayne Barrett, "Romney Campaign, Media Collude in Unprecedented Politicization of Benghazi Attack," TheNation.com, October 22, 2012, http://www.thenation.com/article/170742/romney-campaign-media-collude-unprecedented-politicization-benghazi-attack#.

35. Scott Shane, "Clearing the Record About Benghazi," New York Times, October 17, 2012, http://www.nytimes.com/2012/10/18/us/politics/questions-and-answers-on-the-benghazi-attack.html.

36. *Hannity*, Fox News Channel, October 10, 2012. Nexis.

37. *On the Record with Greta Van Susteren*, Fox News Channel, October 10, 2012. Nexis.

38. David Brock, Ari Rabin-Havt, and Media Matters for America, *The Fox Effect: How Roger Ailes Turned a Network into a Propaganda Machine* (New York: Anchor Books, 2007).

39. Ibid.

40 David Limbaugh, "War On Terror? What War?" January 4, 2010, DavidLimbaugh.com, http://www.davidlimbaugh.com/mt/archives/2010/01/new_column_war.html.

41. *2016: Obama's America* (Rocky Mountain Pictures, 2012). http://mediamatters.org/blog/2012/09/12/embassy-attack-politics-straight-from-the-fever/189851.

42. *Hannity*, Fox News Channel, October 11, 2012. Nexis.

43. "Complete transcript of the Hofstra presidential debate," Newsday.com, October 16, 2012. http://www.newsday.com/elections/complete-transcript-of-the-hofstra-presidential-debate-1.4123391?print=true.

44. "Second Presidential Debate Full Transcript," ABCNews.com, October 17, 2012. http://abcnews.go.com/Politics/OTUS/2012-presidential-debate-full-transcript-oct-16/story?id=17493848&singlePage=true.

45. "Remarks by the President on the Deaths of U.S. Embassy Staff in Libya," WhiteHouse.gov, September 12, 2012, http://www.whitehouse.gov/the-press-office/2012/09/12/remarks-president-deaths-us-embassy-staff-libya.

46. "Obama official: Benghazi was a terrorist attack," The Cable, ForeignPolicy.com, September 19, 2012. http://thecable.foreignpolicy.com/posts/2012/09/19/obama_official_benghazi_was_a_terrorist_attack.

47. "Transcript: President Obama's Convention Speech," NPR.org, September 6, 2012. http://www.npr.org/2012/09/06/160713941/transcript-president-obamas-convention-speech.

48. "Remarks by President Obama and Prime Minister Cameron of the United Kingdom in Joint Press Conference," WhiteHouse.gov, May 13, 2013. http://www.whitehouse.gov/the-press-office/2013/05/13/remarks-president-obama-and-prime-minister-cameron-united-kingdom-joint-.

49. *On the Record with Greta Van Susteren*, Fox News Channel, October 16, 2012. http://mediamatters.org/blog/2012/10/16/transcript-truthers-conservatives-deny-obama-ca/190677.

50. Justin Berrier, "Fox Spent Four Hours Trying To Explain Away Obama's 'Acts Of Terror' Comments," MediaMatters.org, October 22, 2012. http://mediamatters.org/research/2012/10/22/fox-spent-four-hours-trying-to-explain-away-oba/190834.

51. *Fox News Sunday*, Fox Broadcasting Co., October 21, 2012. http://mediamatters.org/blog/2012/10/21/fox-news-sunday-dishonestly-cuts-up-obamas-acts/190797.

52. *America's Newsroom*, Fox News Channel, October 17, 2012. http://mediamatters.org/blog/2012/10/17/transcript-trutherism-jumps-to-foxs-straight-ne/190704.

53. *Fox & Friends*, Fox News Channel, October 17, 2012. http://mediamatters.org/blog/2012/10/17/fox-cherry-picks-obama-quotes-to-rehabilitate-r/190688.

54. *America Live*, Fox News Channel, May 13, 2013. http://mediamatters.org/blog/2013/05/13/fox-and-issa-claim-theres-a-difference-between/194050.

55. "'This Week' Transcript: U.S. Ambassador to the United Nations Susan Rice," ABCNews.com, September 16, 2012. http://abcnews.go.com/Politics/week-transcript-us-ambassador-united-nations-susan-rice/story?id=17240933#.UHYeQxXA_dm.

56. *The Five*, Fox News Channel, September 21, 2012. http://mediamatters.org/research/2012/09/26/myths-and-facts-about-the-benghazi-attack-and-p/190150.

57. Lucy Madison, "Graham: Susan Rice 'disconnected to reality,' doesn't 'deserve' promotion," CBSNews.com, November 14, 2012. http://www.cbsnews.com/8301-250_162-57549819/graham-susan-rice-disconnected-to-reality-doesnt-deserve-promotion/.

58. *Anderson Cooper 360*, CNN, November 14, 2012. http://transcripts.cnn.com/TRANSCRIPTS/1211/14/acd.02.html.

59. *Fox & Friends*, Fox News Channel, November 14, 2012. http://www.mediaite.com/tv/sen-john-mccain-i-will-do-everything-in-my-power-to-block-susan-rice-from-being-sec-of-state/.

60. Paul Richter, "GOP senators unswayed after meeting with Susan Rice," *Los Angeles Times*, November 27, 2012. http://articles.latimes.com/2012/nov/27/nation/la-na-susan-rice-20121128.

61. The Situation Room, CNN, November 28, 2012. http://transcripts.cnn.com/TRANSCRIPTS/1211/28/sitroom.02.html.

62. David Kirkpatrick, "Election-Year Stakes Overshadow Nuances of Libya Investigation." *New York Times*, October 15, 2012. http://www.nytimes.com/2012/10/16/world/africa/election-year-stakes-overshadow-nuances-of-benghazi-investigation.html.

63. Michael Calderone, "Reuters' Early Report Of Protesters At Libya Attack Raises Questions," HuffingtonPost.com, October 15, 2012. http://www.huffingtonpost.com/2012/10/15/reuters-libya-attack_n_1967494.html.

64. David Ignatius, "CIA documents supported Susan Rice's description of Benghazi attacks," *Washington Post*, October 19, 2012. http://www.washingtonpost.com/opinions/benghazi-attack-becomes-political-ammunition/2012/10/19/e1ad82ae-1a2d-11e2-bd10-5ff056538b7c_story.html?hpid=z2.

65. Sabrina Siddiqui, "John McCain, Lindsey Graham Stand By Susan Rice Claims Despite Release Of Benghazi Emails," HuffingtonPost.com, May 21, 2013. http://www.huffingtonpost.com/2013/05/21/john-mccain-susan-rice_n_3314212.html.

66. *On the Record with Greta Van Susteren*, Fox News Channel, May 22, 2013. http://video.foxnews.com/v/2404842493001/graham-rice-wont-get-an-apology-shell-get-a-subpoena/.

67. Scott Wilson and Karen DeYoung, "Petraeus's role in drafting Benghazi talking points raises questions," *Washington Post*, May 21, 2013. http://articles.washingtonpost.com/2013-05-21/politics/39420257_1_petraeus-benghazi-attack-house-permanent-select-committee.

68. *Ibid.*

69. "CIA talking points for Susan Rice called Benghazi attack 'spontaneously inspired' by protests," CBSNews.com, November 15, 2012. http://www.cbsnews.com/8301-505263_162-57550337/cia-talking-points-for-susan-rice-called-benghazi-attack-spontaneously-inspired-by-protests/.

70. *On the Record with Greta Van Susteren*, Fox News Channel, November 14, 2012. http://www.foxnews.com/on-air/on-the-record/index.html#/v/1969794239001/mccain-goes-after-obamas-failed-leadership/?playlist_id=86925.

71. Steve Holland, "McCain says al Qaeda might try to tip U.S. election," Reuters.com, March 14, 2008. http://www.reuters.com/article/2008/03/14/us-usa-politics-mccain-idUSN1418633520080314?i=4.

72. Eric Schmitt, "Petraeus Says U.S. Tried to Avoid Tipping Off Terrorists After Libya Attack," *New York Times*, November 16, 2012. http://www.nytimes.com/2012/11/17/world/africa/benghazi-not-petraeus-affair-is-focus-at-hearings.html?_r=2&pagewanted=all&.

73. Ibid.

74. Ken Dilanian and Christi Parsons, "Mistaken Benghazi claim came from CIA, emails show," *Los Angeles Times*, May 15, 2013. http://articles.latimes.com/2013/may/15/nation/la-na-benghazi-emails-20130516.

75. *Happening Now*, Fox News Channel, November 26, 2012. http://mediamatters.org/blog/2012/11/26/foreign-policys-tom-ricks-appears-on-fox-news-t/191509.

76. *Washington Post* editorial board, "Mr. Burton Should Step Aside," *Washington Post*, March 20, 1997. Nexis.

77. Dan Balz, "Experience Beats Money In Calif. Primary," *Washington Post*, June 4, 1998. http://www.washingtonpost.com/wp-srv/politics/campaigns/keyraces98/stories/keycampaign060498.htm.

78. Kate McCarthy, "Rep. Darrell Issa: Obama Not 'Personally Corrupt,'" ABCNews.com, November 8, 2010. http://abcnews.go.com/blogs/politics/2010/11/rep-darrell-issa-obama-not-personally-corrupt/.

79. Michael Teitelbaum, "Immigration Issue Again Draws In-House Rivals to Utah Lawmaker," Congressional Quarterly, June 7, 2007. http://www.nytimes.com/cq/2007/06/07/cq_2852.html.

80. *Fox & Friends*, Fox News Channel, May 8, 2013. http://mediamatters.org/blog/2013/05/06/fox-denies-political-nature-of-gops-focus-on-be/193919.

81. *The Daily Rundown*, MSNBC, May 8, 2013. http://maddowblog.msnbc.com/_news/2013/05/08/18125854-i-feel-like-i-know-what-happened-in-benghazi?lite.

82. Dana Milbank, "Letting us in on a secret," *Washington Post*, October 10, 2012. http://articles.washingtonpost.com/2012-10-10/opinions/35501217_1_benghazi-darrell-issa-security-lapses.

83. Joshua Hersh, "Jason Chaffetz Has No Regrets On Sensitive Libya Documents Dump," HuffingtonPost.com, October 23, 2012. http://www.huffingtonpost.com/2012/10/23/jason-chaffetz-libya-documents_n_2006856.html.

84. Josh Rogin, "Issa's Benghazi document dump exposes several Libyans working with the U.S.," ForeignPolicy.com, October 19, 2012. http://thecable.foreignpolicy.com/posts/2012/10/19/issa_s_benghazi_document_dump_exposes_several_libyans_working_with_the_us.

85. *Ibid.*

86. Joshua Hersh, "Jason Chaffetz Has No Regrets On Sensitive Libya Documents Dump." HuffingtonPost.com, October 23, 2012. http://www.huffingtonpost.com/2012/10/23/jason-chaffetz-libya-documents_n_2006856.html.

87. Josh Rogin, "Dems allege improprieties in GOP Benghazi investigation," The Cable, ForeignPolicy.com, October 9, 2012. http://thecable.foreignpolicy.com/posts/2012/10/09/dems_allege_improprieties_in_gop_benghazi_investigation.

88. Elias Groll, "Meet the combatants in today's big Benghazi hearing," The Cable, ForeignPolicy.com, May 8, 2013. http://thecable.foreignpolicy.com/posts/2013/05/08/meet_the_combatants_in_todays_big_benghazi_hearing_0.

89. *On the Record with Greta Van Susteren*, Fox News Channel, December 17, 2012. http://mediamatters.org/research/2012/12/18/fox-news-accuses-hillary-clinton-of-faking-conc/191904.

90. *The Five*, Fox News Channel, January 5, 2013. http://mediamatters.org/blog/2013/01/05/foxs-the-five-tries-to-defend-its-mockery-of-cl/192049.

91. *Special Report with Bret Baier*, Fox News Channel, December 19, 2012. http://mediamatters.org/blog/2012/12/20/foxs-evening-shows-mock-hillary-clintons-concus/191920.

92. *New York Post* staff, "Hillary Clinton's head fake," New York Post, December 18, 2012. http://www.nypost.com/p/news/opinion/editorials/hillary_clinton_head_fake_zVFpp9BtsPYVvtmvYp3FWO.

93. Caitlin Ginley, " 'Did She Fake It?': LA Times Mainstreams Clinton Concussion Conspiracy," MediaMatters.org, December 20, 2012. http://mediamatters.org/blog/2012/12/20/did-she-fake-it-la-times-mainstreams-clinton-co/191928.

94. Julian Pecquet, "State Dept. slams John Bolton for suggesting Clinton faked illness," TheHill.com, December 18, 2012, http://thehill.com/blogs/global-affairs/un-treaties/273495-state-department-slams-john-boltons-wild-speculation-that-clinton-faking-illness-.

95. "Hillary Clinton hospitalized after doctors discover blood clot," NBCNews.com, December 31, 2012. http://www.nbcnews.com/health/hillary-clinton-hospitalized-after-doctors-discover-blood-clot-1C7779554.

96. @MattMackowiak, Twitter.com, December 30, 2012. https://twitter.com/MattMackowiak/statuses/285564257326739457.

97. "Hillary Clinton Hearing on Benghazi," CNN.com, January 23, 2013. http://transcripts.cnn.com/TRANSCRIPTS/1301/23/se.01.html.

98. *Ibid.*

99. Andy Newbold, "Fox's Ingraham Suggests Clinton Was 'Lip-Synching Crying' At Benghazi Hearing," MediaMatters.org, January 23, 2013. http://mediamatters.org/blog/2013/01/23/foxs-ingraham-suggests-clinton-was-lip-synching/192355.

100. *The Rush Limbaugh Show*, Premiere Radio Networks, January 23, 2013. http://mediamatters.org/video/2013/01/23/limbaugh-at-benghazi-hearing-clinton-opened-up/192361.

101. McKay Coppins, "Ron Johnson: Hillary Clinton Planned To Get Emotional To Evade Questions," BuzzFeed.com, January 23, 2013. http://www.buzzfeed.com/mckaycoppins/ron-johnson-hillary-clinton-planned-to-get-emotio.

102. *The Sean Hannity Show*, Premiere Radio Networks, January 23, 2013, http://mediamatters.org/video/2013/01/23/hannity-sec-clintons-anger-at-benghazi-hearing/192365.

103. *Glenn Beck*, CNN Headline News, January 8, 2008. http://mediamatters.org/research/2008/01/09/media-figures-claimed-clintons-emotional-moment/142093.

104. Terry Krepel, "Right-Wing Media Responds To Clinton's Libya Statement with Sexist Attacks," MediaMatters.org, October 18, 2012. http://mediamatters.org/research/2012/10/18/right-wing-media-responds-to-clintons-libya-sta/190751.

105. *Special Report with Bret Baier*, Fox News Channel, January 23, 2013. http://www.foxnews.com/on-air/special-report-bret-baier/2013/01/23/hume-clinton-dominated-benghazi-hearings.

106. Emily Arrowood, "Conservative Media Selectively Crop Panetta's Congressional Testimony To Attack Obama On Benghazi," MediaMatters.org, February 7, 2013. http://mediamatters.org/blog/2013/02/07/conservative-media-selectively-crop-panettas-co/192580.

107. Michael Goodwin, "Nobody wake Barack," *New York Post*, February 20, 2013. http://nypost.com/2013/02/10/nobody-wake-barack/.

108. Michael Barone, "Obama's weak policies increase rather than lessen risk of war," *Washington Examiner*, February 9, 2013. http://washingtonexaminer.com/article/2521033.

109. *America's Newsroom*, Fox News Channel, May 9, 2013. http://mediamatters.org/blog/2013/05/09/foxs-crowley-revisits-debunked-myth-that-obama/193990.

110. Gen. Martin Dempsey, Testimony before the Senate Armed Services Committee, February 7, 2013. http://mediamatters.org/research/2013/02/11/facts-mia-in-right-wing-medias-latest-benghazi/192620.

111. Donna Cassata and Richard Lardner, "Leon Panetta Benghazi Testimony: Defense Secretary Explains Military Response In Libya Attack," Associated Press, February 7, 2013. http://www.huffingtonpost.com/2013/02/07/leon-panetta-benghazi_n_2638283.html.

112. *CNN Newsroom*, CNN, January 23, 2013. http://edition.cnn.com/TRANSCRIPTS/1301/23/cnr.02.html.

113. "Hicks: Clinton called me at 2 a.m. the night of Benghazi," CBSNews.com, May 8, 2013. http://www.cbsnews.com/video/watch/?id=50146433n.

114. *Fox & Friends*, Fox News Channel, May 30, 2013. http://mediamatters.org/blog/2013/05/30/fox-drags-another-obama-official-into-manufactu/194266.

115. Adam Housley, "Special forces could've responded to Benghazi attack, whistle-blower tells Fox News." FoxNews.com, April 30, 2013.

http://www.foxnews.com/politics/2013/04/30/special-ops-benghazi-whistleblower-tells-fox-news-government-could-have/.

116. Ashley Fantz, "Panetta, Dempsey defend U.S. response to Benghazi attack,." CNN.com, February 13, 2013. http://www.cnn.com/2013/02/07/us/panetta-benghazi-hearing.

117. Peggy Noonan, "The Inconvenient Truth About Benghazi," *Wall Street Journal*, May 10, 2013. http://online.wsj.com/article/SB10001424127887324244304578473533965297330.html?mod=WSJ_article_RecentColumns_Declarations.

118. Jake Tapper and Dana Bash, "Former deputy chief of mission in Libya: U.S. military assets told to stand down," CNN.com, May 7, 2013. http://www.cnn.com/2013/05/06/politics/benghazi-whistleblower/index.html.

119. Max Fisher, "Robert Gates on Benghazi: 'There just wasn't time,' " WashingtonPost.com, May 13, 2013. http://www.washingtonpost.com/blogs/worldviews/wp/2013/05/13/robert-gates-on-benghazi-there-just-wasnt-time/.

120. *Ibid.*

121. Leon Panetta, "Statement on the Attacks on the US Facilities in Benghazi, Libya before the Senate Armed Services Committee," Defense.gov, February 7, 2013. http://www.defense.gov/speeches/speech.aspx?speechid=1748.

122. "Interim Progress Report for the Members of the House Republican Conference on the Events Surrounding the September 11, 2012 Terrorist Attacks in Benghazi, Libya," House.gov, April 23, 2013. http://oversight.house.gov/wp-content/uploads/2013/04/Libya-Progress-Report-Final-1.pdf.

123. *Ibid.*

124. *Ibid.*

125. Elise Labott, "Clinton: I'm responsible for diplomats' security," CNN.com, October 16, 2012. http://www.cnn.com/2012/10/15/us/clinton-benghazi.

126. Deirdre Walsh and Jill Dougherty, "House GOP Benghazi report says Clinton signed off on security reduction," Security Clearance, CNN.com, April 23, 2013. http://security.blogs.cnn.com/2013/04/23/house-gop-benghazi-report-says-clinton-signed-off-on-security-reduction/.

127. Stephanie Condon, "House GOP faults Clinton, State Dept for Benghazi security," CBSNews.com, April 23, 2013. http://www.cbsnews.com/8301-250_162-57581052/house-gop-faults-clinton-state-dept-for-benghazi-security/.

128. Kevin Cirilli, "Darrell Issa: Hillary Clinton 'wrong' on Benghazi," Politico.
com, April 24, 2013. http://www.politico.com/story/2013/04/darrell-issa-
hillary-clinton-benghazi-90560.html.

129. Glenn Kessler, "Issa's absurd claim that Clinton's 'signature' means she
personally approved it," The Fact Checker, *Washington Post*, April 26, 2013. http://
www.washingtonpost.com/blogs/fact-checker/post/issas-absurd-claim-that-
clintons-signature-means-she-personally-approved-it/2013/04/25/58c2f5b4-
adf8-11e2-a986-eec837b1888b_blog.html.

130. *Investor's Business Daily* editorial board, "Hillary Clinton Lied, And Four In
Benghazi Died," Investor's Business Daily, April 24, 2013. http://news.investors.
com/print/ibd-editorials/042413-653232-house-report-details-hillary-clinton-
benghazi-lies.aspx.

131. Guy Benson, "Benghazi Report: Hillary Approved Reduced Security
Measures, Contradicting Previous Testimony," Townhall.com, April 24,
2013. http://townhall.com/tipsheet/guybenson/2013/04/24/benghazi-
report-hillary-approved-reduced-security-measures-contradicting-her-
testimony-n1576710.

132. Julian Pecquet, "Benghazi Bombshell Drops On Obama, Hillary,"
FoxNation.com, April 23, 2013. http://nation.foxnews.com/benghazi-
attacks/2013/04/23/benghazi-bombshell-drops-obama-hillary.

133. Sen. Rand Paul, "The moment of responsibility for Hillary Clinton,"
Washington Times, May 10, 2013. http://www.washingtontimes.com/news/2013/
may/10/the-moment-of-responsibility-for-hillary-clinton/?page=1.

134. John Avlon, "With Benghazi Video, Karl Rove Kicks Off 2016 With Hillary
Clinton Hit," TheDailyBeast.com, May 13, 2013. http://www.thedailybeast.
com/articles/2013/05/13/with-benghazi-video-karl-rove-kicks-off-2016-with-
hillary-clinton-hit.html.

135. "Politico's Allen Lets One Slip on Republican's Motives Behind Benghazi
Scandal-Mongering," CrooksAndLiars.com, May 30, 2013. http://videocafe.
crooksandliars.com/heather/politicos-allen-lets-one-slip-republicans.

136. Glenn Kessler, "Issa's absurd claim that Clinton's 'signature' means she personally approved it," The Fact Checker, *Washington Post*, April 26, 2013. http://www.washingtonpost.com/blogs/fact-checker/post/issas-absurd-claim-that-clintons-signature-means-she-personally-approved-it/2013/04/25/58c2f5b4-adf8-11e2-a986-eec837b1888b_blog.html.

137. John McCain, Lindsey Graham and Kelly Ayotte, "Critical questions still unanswered on Benghazi," *Washington Times*, December 22, 2012, http://www.washingtontimes.com/news/2012/dec/22/critical-questions-still-unanswered-on-benghazi/.

138. "Interim Progress Report for the Members of the House Republican Conference on the Events Surrounding the September 11, 2012 Terrorist Attacks in Benghazi, Libya," House.gov, April 23, 2013. http://oversight.house.gov/wp-content/uploads/2013/04/Libya-Progress-Report-Final-1.pdf.

139. Victoria Toensing, "Administration Relying on Shoddy Benghazi Report to Absolve Itself of Blame," WeeklyStandard.com, May 12, 2013. http://www.weeklystandard.com/blogs/administration-relying-shoddy-benghazi-report-absolve-itself-blame_722379.html.

140. "Barack and a Hard Place," *The O'Reilly Factor*, Fox News Channel, May 14, 2013. Nexis.

141. State Department Accountability Review Board report, December 18, 2012. http://www.state.gov/documents/organization/202446.pdf.

142. *Ibid.*

143. "Kerry clears 4 State staffers put on leave over Benghazi attack to return to work," CBSNews.com, August 20, 2013. http://www.cbsnews.com/8301-250_162-57599324/kerry-clears-4-state-staffers-put-on-leave-over-benghazi-attack-to-return-to-work/.

144. John Hudson, "Issa and Pickering clash over new Benghazi hearing," The Cable, ForeignPolicy.com, May 15, 2013. http://thecable.foreignpolicy.com/posts/2013/05/15/issa_and_pickering_clash_over_new_benghazi_hearing.

145. "Issa Statement on Secretary Kerry's Decision Not to Pursue Discipline for any Officials in Benghazi Probe," Committee on Oversight and Government Reform, August 20, 2013. http://oversight.house.gov/release/issa-statement-on-secretary-kerrys-decision-to-not-to-pursue-discipline-for-any-officials-in-benghazi-probe/.

146. *Fox & Friends*, Fox News Channel, September 4, 2013, http://mediamatters.org/blog/2013/09/04/fox-continues-to-push-falsehood-about-state-dep/195712.

147. Sharyl Attkisson, "House investigators talking to new Benghazi whistleblowers," CBSNews.com, April 17, 2013. http://www.cbsnews.com/8301-250_162-57580105/house-investigators-talking-to-new-benghazi-whistleblowers/.

148. Seth Mnookin, "More embarrassing anti-vaccine reporting from CBS News's Sharyl Attkisson," SethMnookin.com, March 31, 2011. http://sethmnookin.com/2011/03/31/more-embarrassing-anti-vaccine-reporting-from-cbs-newss-sharyl-attkisson/.

149. "Issa: Oversight Committee to Resume Benghazi Hearings Next Month," Oversight.House.gov, April 24, 2013. http://oversight.house.gov/release/issa-oversight-committee-to-resume-benghazi-hearings-next-month/.

150. James Rosen, "Obama administration officials threatened whistle-blowers on Benghazi, lawyer says," FoxNews.com, April 29, 2013. http://www.foxnews.com/politics/2013/04/29/obama-administration-officials-have-threatened-whistle-blowers-on-benghazi/.

151. "News Conference by the President," WhiteHouse.gov, April 30, 2013. http://www.whitehouse.gov/the-press-office/2013/04/30/news-conference-president.

152. "Fox News All-Stars," *Special Report with Bret Baier*, Fox News Channel, April 30, 2013. Nexis.

153. Simon Maloy, "Victoria Toensing Should Confer With Her Client," MediaMatters.org, May 11, 2013. http://mediamatters.org/blog/2013/05/11/victoria-toensing-should-confer-with-her-client/194019.

154. Testimony before the House Oversight Committee, May 8, 2013. http://mediamatters.org/blog/2013/05/09/the-benghazi-whistleblower-cover-up-that-wasnt/193984.

155. Simon Maloy, "Victoria Toensing Should Confer With Her Client," MediaMatters.org, May 11, 2013. http://mediamatters.org/blog/2013/05/11/victoria-toensing-should-confer-with-her-client/194019.

156. Karen DeYoung, "State Department disputes diplomat's charges of retaliation," *Washington Post*, May 8, 2013. http://www.washingtonpost.com/world/national-security/state-department-disputes-diplomats-charges-of-retaliation/2013/05/08/60ee1cd8-b833-11e2-b94c-b684dda07add_story.html.

157. Ben Shapiro, "Whistleblower: Hilary's State Dept. Told Me Not To Talk To Congress," Breitbart.com, May 8, 2013. http://www.breitbart.com/Big-Government/2013/05/08/Whistleblower-state-dept-censor.

158. Scott Shane, Jeremy W. Peters, and Eric Schmitt, "Diplomat Says Questions Over Benghazi Led to Demotion," *New York Times*, May 8, 2013. http://www.nytimes.com/2013/05/09/us/politics/official-offers-account-from-libya-of-benghazi-attack.html?hp&_r=0.

159. Dana Milbank, "Whistleblower's yarn fails to tie Benghazi lapses to politics," *Washington Post*, May 8, 2013. http://articles.washingtonpost.com/2013-05-08/opinions/39115035_1_darrell-issa-benghazi-mortar-attack.

160. Simon Maloy, "Cheryl Mills' (Non) Threatening Phone Call," MediaMatters.org, May 11, 2013. http://mediamatters.org/blog/2013/05/11/cheryl-mills-non-threatening-phone-call/194020.

161. Media Matters staff, "Who Are The Right-Wing Media's Benghazi Lawyers Victoria Toensing And Joseph diGenova," MediaMatters.org, April 30, 2013. http://mediamatters.org/research/2013/04/30/who-are-the-right-wing-medias-benghazi-lawyers/193842.

162. Noah Rothman, "Eric Bolling Explodes At Geraldo Over Obama's Response To Benghazi, Hangs Up Mid-Interview," Mediaite.com, http://www.mediaite.com/online/eric-bolling-explodes-at-geraldo-over-obamas-response-to-benghazi-hangs-up-mid-interview/.

163. Arnold Ahlert, "Blow-by-Blow: How Obama & Hillary Left Americans to Die," FrontPageMag.com, May 9, 2013. http://frontpagemag.com/2013/arnold-ahlert/blow-by-blow-how-obama-hillary-left-americans-to-die/.

164. Katie Pavlich, "Hillary Clinton's Big Benghazi Lie," Townhall.com, May 8, 2013. http://townhall.com/tipsheet/katiepavlich/2013/05/08/hillary-clintons-big-benghazi-lie-n1591097.

165. *America Live*, Fox News Channel, October 10, 2012. http://mediamatters.org/research/2012/10/10/foxs-mcfarland-invents-facts-to-accuse-obama-ad/190530.

166. *Fox & Friends*, Fox News Channel, October 25, 2012. http://mediamatters.org/research/2012/10/26/foxs-new-low-accusing-obama-admin-of-abandoning/190948.

167. State Department Accountability Review Board report, December 18, 2012, http://www.state.gov/documents/organization/202446.pdf.

168. James Rosen and Chad Pergram, "Clinton sought end-run around counterterrorism bureau on night of Benghazi attack, witness will say," FoxNews.com, May 6, 2013. http://www.foxnews.com/politics/2013/05/06/clinton-sought-end-run-around-counterterrorism-bureau-on-night-benghazi-attack/.

169. Becky Bowers, "Jason Chaffetz says Americans were ready to save men 'getting killed' in Benghazi were told to stand down," PolitiFact.com, May 14, 2013. http://www.politifact.com/truth-o-meter/statements/2013/may/14/jason-chaffetz/rep-jason-chaffetz-says-special-forces-ready-save-/.

170. Sharyl Attkisson, "Diplomat: U.S. Special Forces told 'you can't go' to Benghazi during attacks," CBSNews.com, May 16, 2013. http://www.cbsnews.com/8301-250_162-57583014/diplomat-u.s-special-forces-told-you-cant-go-to-benghazi-during-attacks/.

171. Madeleine Morgenstern, "Benghazi Witness On Stand-Down Order: 'First Time In My Career That A Diplomat Has More Balls Than Somebody In The Military," TheBlaze.com, May 8, 2013. http://www.theblaze.com/stories/2013/05/08/benghazi-witness-on-stand-down-order-first-time-in-my-career-that-a-diplomat-has-more-balls-than-somebody-in-the-military/.

172. "Issa Statement on Benghazi Whistleblower Hearing and Unanswered Questions," Oversight.House.gov, May 8, 2013. http://oversight.house.gov/release/issa-statement-on-benghazi-whistleblower-hearing-and-unanswered-questions/.

173. *Fox & Friends*, Fox News Channel, May 9, 2013. http://mediamatters.org/blog/2013/05/09/fox-ignores-benghazi-witness-testimony-proving/193981.

174. Zachary Pleat, "No Benghazi 'Stand Down' Order Was Given: Another Fox Narrative Falls Apart," MediaMatters.org, June 27, 2013. http://mediamatters.org/blog/2013/06/27/no-benghazi-stand-down-order-was-given-another/194644.

175. Leon Panetta, "Statement on the Attacks on the US Facilities in Benghazi, Libya before the Senate Armed Services Committee," Defense.gov, February 7, 2013. http://www.defense.gov/speeches/speech.aspx?speechid=1748.

176. Testimony before the Senate Budget Committee, June 12, 2013. http://www.c-spanvideo.org/event/220017.

177. "Officer: No Libya stand-down order," Associated Press, June 27, 2013. http://azstarnet.com/news/national/govt-and-politics/officer-no-libya-stand-down-order/article_3ebd5c58-41ab-577c-98ac-331d752cc9c4.html.

178. "Report: Marine commander says no stand-down orer in Benghazi attack," UPI, July 31, 2013. http://www.upi.com/Top_News/US/2013/07/31/Report-Marine-commander-says-no-stand-down-order-in-Benghazi-attack/UPI-95121375252200/?spt=hs&or=tn.

179. Zachary Pleat, "Fox Anchor Bret Baier Botches Benghazi Timeline," MediaMatters.org, May 7, 2013. http://mediamatters.org/blog/2013/05/07/fox-anchor-bret-baier-botches-benghazi-timeline/193937.

180. Jonathan Karl, "Exclusive: Benghazi Talking Points Underwent 12 Revisins, Scrubbed of Terror Reference," ABCNews.com, May 10, 2013. http://abcnews.go.com/blogs/politics/2013/05/exclusive-benghazi-talking-points-underwent-12-revisions-scrubbed-of-terror-references/.

181. "Press Briefing by Press Secretary Jay Carney, 11/28/2012," WhiteHouse.gov, November 28, 2012. http://www.whitehouse.gov/the-press-office/2012/11/28/press-briefing-press-secretary-jay-carney-11282012.

182. "Benghazi Hearings," *Hannity*, Fox News Channel, May 10, 2013. Nexis.

183. Benjamin Bell, "Sen. John McCain Asserts Benghazi 'Cover-Up,' " ABCNews.com, May 12, 2013. http://abcnews.go.com/blogs/politics/2013/05/sen-john-mccain-asserts-benghazi-cover-up/.

184. *Ibid.*

185. "Administration Statements on the Attack in Benghazi," NYTimes.com, September 27, 2012. http://www.nytimes.com/interactive/2012/09/27/world/africa/administration-statements-on-the-attack-in-benghazi.html.

186. Jake Tapper, "CNN exclusive: White House email contradicts Benghazi leaks," CNN.com, May 14, 2013, http://thelead.blogs.cnn.com/2013/05/14/cnn-exclusive-white-house-email-contradicts-benghazi-leaks/.

187. *Ibid.*

188. Josh Marshall, "The Latest Turn of the Scre," TalkingPointsMemo.com, May 20, 2013. http://talkingpointsmemo.com/archives/2013/05/the_latest_turn_of_the_screw.php.

189. Joe Strupp, "Media Observers on ABC's Jonathan Karl Benghazi Talking Points Story: 'Sloppy' And 'Inaccurate,' " MediaMatters.org, May 16, 2013. http://mediamatters.org/blog/2013/05/16/media-observers-on-abcs-jonathan-karl-benghazi/194095.

190. Mark Landler, Eric Schmidt, Michael Shear, "Early E-Mails on Benghazi Show Internal Divisions," *New York Times*, May 15, 2013. http://www.nytimes.com/2013/05/16/us/politics/e-mails-show-jostling-over-benghazi-talking-points.html?pagewanted=all.

191. *CBS Evening News with Scott Pelley*, CBS, May 16, 2013. http://mediamatters.org/video/2013/05/16/cbs-evening-news-highlights-collapse-of-right-w/194116.

192. *New Haven Register* staff, "Anti-Obama Protestors Rally on New Haven I-95 Overpass," August 30, 2013. http://www.nhregister.com/government-and-politics/20130830/anti-obama-protesters-rally-on-new-haven-i-95-overpass.

193. Adam K. Raymond, "The Story Behind the 'Overpasses For Obama Impeachment' Movement," *New York*, August 23, 2013. http://nymag.com/daily/intelligencer/2013/08/behind-overpasses-obama-impeachment-interview.html.

194. Jeremy Herb, "GOP Sen. Inhofe: Obama could be impeached over Benghazi 'cover-up' " DEFCON Hill, TheHill.com, May 10, 2013. http://thehill.com/blogs/defcon-hill/policy-and-strategy/299009-inhofe-obama-could-be-impeached-over-benghazi

195. Zachary Pleat, "CNN Benghazi Special Pushes Debunked And Deceptive Claims," MediaMatters.org, August 7, 2013. http://mediamatters.org/research/2013/08/07/cnn-benghazi-special-pushes-debunked-and-decept/195272.

196. "Benghazi attack: Ahmed Abu Khattala, the head of a Libyan militia, charged," Associated Press, August 6, 2013. http://www.oregonlive.com/today/index.ssf/2013/08/benghazi_attack_ahmed_abu_khat.html.

197. "Remarks by the President at Transfer of Remains Ceremony for Benghazi Victims," WhiteHouse.gov, September 14, 2012, http://www.whitehouse.gov/the-press-office/2012/09/14/remarks-president-transfer-remains-ceremony-benghazi-victims.

198. Robert F. Worth, "Can U.S. Diplomacy Ever Come Out of Its Bunker?" *New York Times Magazine*, November 14, 2012. http://www.nytimes.com/2012/11/18/magazine/christopher-stevens-and-the-problem-of-american-diplomacy.html?pagewanted=all.